Diane Franklin

WARNING!

Reading this book may damage any preconceived notion you have of Diane Franklin as an actress. Do not read this if you wish to continue to believe she is really French, British, a seductress, incredibly naïve, or downright evil! This book will change your mind.

MOST EXCELLENT REVIEWS

Quite honestly one of the BEST biographies I have ever read. When I read this book,... I felt I time warped back to the 80's and experiences all those great moments once again, but this time I felt like I was right there with the great star. Diane to this day is still winning the hearts of her fans. After I read her amazing book, she won my heart all over again.

— SCOTT HOFFMAN

The book is a treat for the 80s' film fan with fascinating and delightful reminiscences from an actress who was a major participant of several iconic movies of that decade. A nice blend of biographical anecdotes and life lessons that carries from her childhood to the present. Fully illustrated with never before seen photos rounds out the perfect capsule of a beloved and not forgotten era.

— KEN CHIN

When I was in my 20's in the 1980's, a beautiful brunette graced the screen in the popular romantic comedies of the time. Her name is Diane Franklin, and into the 90's and 2000's I always wondered what happened to my celluloid "dream girl".. This book is an honest tale of how hard work, talent, and perseverance will not only get you through the pitfalls of Hollywood and fame, but how those same beatitudes will form the person that Diane is today. This autobiography is a MUST READ for anyone who would like to pursue a career in entertainment and still take the high road of a fulfilling and rewarding life.

— DAVE ALMEIDA

Diane Franklin is an actress I really admire, which is why I wanted to read her biography. The book was an honest and refreshing read, from start to finish. It starts out with her early childhood, and goes through, and up to her movie career. The book is so descriptive, you feel like Diane is sitting next to you telling her story to you. I highly recommend this book.

— BETH DUTTON GARBERICK

A wonderful read from start to finish. It gave me a fresh prospective of one of my favorite actresses from the 80"s. Bravo to you Diane & Bravo to your wonderful story.

– MICKY ARUTY

....

I read your book and wanted to tell you it's fantastic. You truly are the most excellent babe of the 80s and still going strong today.

– NEIL ALSTATT JR.

....

THE BOOK OF DIANE – A MUST-HAVE! Answering every question you would want to ask and – even more rewardingly – giving insight into where Diane Franklin came from and how she progressed through her life and career, this autobiography will expand the minds and hearts of anyone who has ever been struck by Diane's singular presence. If you've been one of those admirers hoping since 1982 for her story, this book proves to be well worth the wait.

– JASON SIMOS

....

Diane Franklin

· ·

The *Excellent Adventures* of the Last American, French-Exchange *Babe of the 80s*

Official Autobiography Written by

DIANE FRANKLIN

Foreword By

SAVAGE STEVE HOLLAND

Edited by

MICHAEL PICARELLA

Los Angeles, CA

DEDICATION

This book is dedicated to everyone who loves the 80s,
and my wonderful family who inspire me daily.

EDITOR'S NOTE:

Diane Franklin was in one of my favorite comedies of all time—*Better Off Dead* (1985). She was also in the first raunchy teen film I ever saw as a kid—*The Last American Virgin* (1982). At 12, *Virgin* left quite an impression on me.

I never forgot it. And I never forgot Diane.

Intimidating is not the word I'd use to describe my feelings when, as a journalist years later, I was tasked to interview Ms. Franklin for a story. The better word to describe my feelings: *Horrified*. This was, after all, Diane Franklin I was to meet!

Yeah, the first time I met Diane, I was freaked out. I was such a huge fan. But Diane in real life was like the character she played in *Better Off Dead*—so sweet, so funny, so enthusiastic, so positive. I just couldn't be nervous around her. In fact, I felt so comfortable I asked her to play a role in a movie I was directing called *Punchcard Player* (2006). She enthusiastically accepted.

And now I feel privileged once again to play a part in another one of Diane's excellent adventures—her autobiography. Here she exudes the same sweetness, humor, enthusiasm, and positive energy that she showed me when we met and when we were on set. I promise you'll fall in love with Diane Franklin all over again—like you did in the 80s at the movies or in front of your TV sets. Enjoy, enjoy! But I note: While Diane is sweet and nice, if ever you should meet her in real life, please, oh please, keep your "tentacles" to yourself.

Michael Picarella
Editor

FOREWORD

Love Letter To Diane Franklin From Savage Steve

At some point in late 1984, my dream came true. I was given the green light to direct my first feature film, *Better Off Dead*. The movie was really just a string of gags I wrote on bar napkins strung together with non-too-brilliant dialogue along the lines of: "I want my two dollars!" I hoped if I cast the right "dream girl" to play my heroine Monique—a lisping, French exchange student who spoke no English, could throw a mean fastball, completely restore a 1968 S.S. Camaro *and* totally repair my hero Lane's broken heart . . . all in one afternoon—everyone would be so in love with this Monique, they might forgive my script's shortcomings. But who? Who had this kind of bewitching beauty with the necessary girl-next-door charm?

I needed an actress whose smile could simply replace a page of dialogue. My new career hung in the balance! And then Diane Franklin walked in. I remember hearing angels sing. Seriously—when Diane Franklin enters a room it's like, well, a movie. My first impression of Diane was: This is probably how Bill Shakespeare pictured Juliet when he wrote his epic yet tragic love story. Then I remembered I, too, was doing an epic yet tragic love story. Only mine took place in the 80s and involved dancing hamburgers.

This was the first time I'd ever met Diane, but I already knew a couple of things—I was still mad at her for breaking the heart of that poor Gary dude in the movie *The Last American Virgin*. Even scarier, I'd recently seen Diane in a TV movie where she played the part of evil teen temptress Cinni in *SummerGirl* (a precursor to *The Hand That Rocks the Cradle*). In this thriller, she tried to steal Barry Bostwick from poor Kim Darby. Kim Darby was Monique's potential future mother-in-law in my yet-to-be-made movie! This beautiful siren Diane Franklin was so hot, so dangerous, so steamy, and so seductive. How could she possibly be my sweet and precious Monique?

In the casting room that fateful day, Diane Franklin smiled her gazillion-watt smile, then burst out laughing so her amazing, famous curly locks danced around her head, and she reminded me . . . "Ummm, you get that those were just movies, right?" That wasn't really her *right*. More like, "Riiiigghhht?"

It took about one minute to get to know the real Diane—funny, bubbly sweet, giving, creative, talkative, happy, secure, kind, and just plain lovely. On some blog, I've been quoted as describing Diane as "Bambi on acid." And I stand by it. She's doe-like, cute, and lovable almost to an otherworldly degree. Some 25 years later, she still remains a dear friend, and it has been a joy to watch her pass along her amazing gifts to her great kids. I firmly believe all of us in Hollywood will be working for her daughter Olivia one day.

One of the greatest gifts in my life was that Diane Franklin walked into my casting session in 1984 and agreed to star in my first movie. It changed everything, and she helped make *Better Off Dead* the cult classic it is today. I am grateful to Diane and cannot wait to hear the story she has to tell.

With love and respect always,

Savage Steve Holland

TABLE OF CONTENTS

NOTE TO READER

This book was written for adults. If you wish to share it with children under 18 you may want to skip certain chapters. A film-rating symbol is provided at the top of each feature film chapter for your discretion. Enjoy!

PREFACE

I was an 80s teen babe—the hottie, the innocent, the vixen, the sweetheart, the crush, the seductress, the ingénue, the girl you fell in love with. Audiences rooted for me and booed me, adored me and hated me, wanted to be like me or just wanted me. Whether I played the good girl or the bad girl on screen, I always got attention, and I always got the guy. I was an 80s teen babe.

So how did I become a *babe* in the first place? It wasn't maintaining the big hair, balancing on high heels, or even wearing all those sexy clothes. It was the day in, day out, week after week, month after month, year after year pursuit of becoming a professional actress. By the time the 80s rolled around, I had worked long enough in the business to know what to do, and what not to do.

Movies were being made about teens, and lots of teens were watching movies, so the door was wide open for opportunity. I loved to act, wanted to make a living at it, and was going to do it. I just needed a lucky break.

That break hit with the change of stereotypical casting for young girls in film and television. Before the 80s, audiences and studios alike saw underage girls as just kids. But once the 70s faded out, all that changed, and people began to see young teen girls as "babes".

In this book, I will not only share the story of how I became a movie star, but I will also discuss what triggered the change of attitude toward roles that were under 18, and how that directly affected my career. I will also address some of the gritty issues that were expressed alongside the fun and fantasy of 80s teen films, issues which made that decade of cinema so unique. The roles I played expressed the consequences of naiveté or seduction. It was as if 80s teen films were saying to young women, "Wake up! If you aren't more alert, you'll end up in big trouble!"

Finally, I will share the adventure of being an 80s babe actress. Extensive travel, challenging acting roles, and exciting film experiences made it an excellent adventure for me. I am very fortunate to have worked so much as an actress, and to be associated with such an upbeat decade of entertainment. Over the years, I have met so many people who have told me how much they loved the movies I made, how I was a big part in their lives growing up. I hope this book gives better insight into the life of an 80s babe, as well as brings back some *excellent* film and television memories!

With Lots of Love,

Diane Franklin
The Excellent, Last American, French-Exchange Babe of the 80s!

Childhood

A Little Different

"Give her an American name!" my 18-year-old half-sister, Ursula, said to our European immigrant parents.

Thank you, Ursula!

So, on a snowy, February 11th, 1962, my parents decided to name me Diane Alexandra Franklin. I was born with reddish curly hair—like my dad—and was a complete surprise to both my parents, who had been trying to have a baby together for many years. My mother, who was 40 at the time, and my father, 45, were having me late in their lives.

My mother was born a German and raised Protestant, and met my father, an Austrian Jew, in Europe during the 40s. They married before coming to America in 1953 and moved to Queens with my sister before permanently residing in Plainview, Long Island, where I was born and raised. Plainview had a strong Jewish community, and here lived this German woman married to a Jewish man, not too long after WWII. My parents were a little different as well.

Today, having a baby in your 40s might be considered common practice. In the early 60s, however, it was not. It was risky business. During childbirth, my mother was very sick and almost died from kidney failure. As a result, she required hospitalization and certainly could not take care of an infant.

My father worked full time as a purchasing agent for New York Life Insurance, and Ursula was busy finishing high school, so the first couple of months of my life I spent in foster care. After my mother recovered, I was sent home and taken care of by my mother and a nursemaid for almost a year. During that time, my father worked non-stop, and my sister got married and moved away.

Although, I had a slightly rocky start, life stabilized quickly in our modest three-bedroom house. My parents spent a lot of time with me. They read stories to me, played games with me, and took me wherever they went.

When I was very little, I played with my redheaded neighbor, and did tons of drawing—my father would bring home what seemed to be reams of scrap paper from work. I visited animal farms, played with my dog, Heidi, and with my one-eyed hamster, Fluffy. I'd play with stuffed animals, did tons of crafts and danced around the house naked. (I did not like clothes, and would leave a trail up to my room.) I was truly a free spirit.

I have very wonderful memories as a child. I had a happy, energetic nature that my parents valued and nurtured, which certainly helped make childhood an excellent adventure. I was given the freedom to be myself—I was accepted for who I was.

My mother, an at-home mom, raised me to appreciate the simple things in life. I remember her always telling me in broken English to never lose my happiness. I think she said this to me because I was naturally a joyful child, and she didn't want the world to take that spirit away from me. She lived through wartime, and knew the fragility of life, so her advice was that of a grandmother—someone with a bigger perspective. I always felt my mother was very beautiful, had a lot of wisdom, and grace. She was the kind of person who felt that less was more, and instilled in me that the simple things in life were precious.

My father, on the other hand, was not as simple, but loved me to no end. He would tell me that the most important thing in life was to be tolerant. When he was a child in Austria, he was teased for being Jewish, separated from his peers at school the day Hitler came into power, and discovered his parents were killed in a concentration camp when he was just a teen. He was an intense man who lived a very intense life, but he always had time for me. Again, like a grandfather, he was strict, but loving, and he wanted the best for me. He gave me much attention. He instilled in me the importance of commitment and passion. It is from him I learned to love deeply, and to go after my dreams.

So life went along simply for a while until, when I was about 4 years old, my parents discovered something different about me. We had a split-level house, and they would call for me from upstairs to come up. But instead of going up, I'd go down. And when they said my name but a foot or two away, I'd fail to respond altogether.

So, my parents took me to the doctor. The doctor discovered I was completely deaf in my right ear—the nerve, he said, was dead. He told my parents there was nothing that could be done to repair the damage. It didn't bother me, though. Since I had the condition from birth, I knew no different. So I just adjusted my life around it.

I could hear well with my left ear, so I would lean forward in the back seat of the car to hear conversations, or read lips when I was in a crowd. I also got the gist of people's conversations through body language. I tended to look people in the face more, and as a result, I was more connected non-verbally. I later used these skills in my acting communicating more with my eyes, and felt comfortable acting without dialogue.

During those years, I showed other signs of an interest in acting. One time, I stood on a chair in a restaurant and sang loudly to the Muzak. I frequently performed very dramatic dance routines in our living room. There was no judgment or shame, just praise and nurturing of my creative expression. As a result, there was this great sense of freedom to be myself, and what followed was an enjoyment of expressing myself. It was unabashed happiness.

Four years old

Around that time, I remember telling my parents that I wanted to be an actress. I think I got the idea from watching *That Girl*, a television show starring Marlo Thomas. I was a big fan of hers because she had dark hair, which was unusual at the time since most actresses on 60s television shows had blond hair like the women in *Bewitched*, *Green Acres*, and *I Dream of Jeannie*. I identified with Marlo, though. I admired her character's independence. She played an actress who lived in New York, going on auditions all the time. She had the life I wanted. Her character, Anne Marie, was funny and upbeat, and was a positive role model who gave me an idea of what life *could* be like.

At the young age of 4, my parents took me to see a talent agent in New York City for representation. They had no connections and no idea of what they were doing. They just saw a spark in me, and they wanted to help me pursue my dream. Unfortunately, our plans didn't work out so easily. And while we had found an agent, the agent didn't take me on. She said that my hair was too short and curly, and that I should come back when it grew out and I was older. But I wasn't discouraged. I wanted to act. And I was going to find a way to do it no matter what.

Between ages 4 and 10, I took all kinds of classes, not only learning creative skills, but also picking up the disciplines of professional behavior. I studied piano, tap, and began studying ballet until I got on point by the age of 10. Ballet was very confidence-building—painful, but confidence building.

I had a Russian ballet teacher, Nora Kovach, who had been a professional ballerina. She really stressed the importance of good posture and grace. With her I learned to control and isolate my body movement, as well as withstand physical pain, though not excruciating pain, with dignity, which definitely helped with my acting later on. Selecting movement and controlling my body was something I'd use quite often to create characters in my career. Those same tools also came in handy when I had to hold positions for lighting adjustments on set, or when I had to match previous shot stances, or block the movements in a scene. Indeed, ballet helped me with acting.

During this time, I also attended a public elementary school. I was an A/B student who initially struggled with reading—I had problems processing information quickly. I wasn't dyslexic, but I didn't sight read or test very well. As a result, I didn't feel smart growing up, but I started developing the habit of memorizing anything I needed to recite, which eventually helped me when it came time to memorize dialogue in scripts.

I continued living a somewhat idyllic childhood: playing with friends, doing lots of arts, making cartoon strips, writing poems, books and songs, playing board games with my parents, visiting my sister and her family in New Jersey, and spending time in natural surroundings.

My parents often took me to the park or to the beach, or even to the woods. Twice I traveled to Germany to see my grandmother and cousins. And while I never spoke German, I could understand bits and pieces of what my relatives were saying. I think that's when I developed my love of dialects.

I could never hear my own parents' accents, but when we went to visit another country, I could hear the accent distinctly. My role as Monique Junet in *Better Off Dead* was directly influenced by a trip to Quebec, Canada, when I was 9. The French language fascinated me, and I spoke French gibberish throughout the trip. At least *I* knew what I was saying.

In the summer of my tenth year, my parents sent me to the Usdan Center for the Creative and Performing Arts in Long Island. It was a beautiful day camp for 10- to 18-year-olds, nestled in the deep woods.

I chose to study dance and painting for the summer rather than acting, mainly due to the fact that, back in the 70s, agents and managers generally discouraged acting classes. Technique was thought to interfere with a child's natural way of being. I remember thinking—even at such a young age—if I was going to be a good actress and if I wasn't going to take acting classes, then I'd need to *do*, not pretend to do. So I took classes in things I wanted to experience in life.

But while I was attending this camp, I heard about some auditions for a big talent show. It was highly competitive. At 10 years old, however, I didn't care how competitive it was. I just wanted to audition and decided I was going to sing one of my favorite songs; "Harper Valley PTA."

After auditioning against hundreds of other kids, the judges chose my solo for the talent show to be accompanied by the camp's band. I couldn't believe it. Dressed in my red and white polka-dotted skirt that my mom had made me, there on a big stage, I sang my heart out with a live high school band. I have to say—if there was ever a big moment in my childhood, that was it. Moments like those showed me that I could be a performer, and it showed my parents my commitment and devotion for performing.

And so, at the beginning of the 4th grade, I tried again to get into the business of acting.

Pre-Teen 10 -12
Modeling and Commercials

Modeling

At age 10, I begged my parents to set up a meeting with a new agent. Once again we returned to New York City.

My mother and father had no idea how to get into the entertainment business, so unfortunately we fell prey to a so-called talent agency that charged us for auditions, classes, pictures, and the like. After being with this agency for about a month, we discovered the people there were scam artists.

Through word of mouth, we found the name of a real talent manager. Her name was Barbara Jarrett, and she ran her own management company on the Upper East Side. It was a small group that focused mostly on youth, and handled a couple dozen clients, including Vincent Spano (*Rumble Fish, Oscar*), Elisabeth Shue (*Back to the Future Part II, Leaving Las Vegas*), and Lori Loughlin (*Full House, Rad*). In the early 70s, we were all just starting our careers in New York.

After 15 minutes with Barbara in her Upper East Side apartment, she decided to take me on. I was thrilled. I remember I had to contain myself from jumping all over her furniture. Barbara was a fast-talking, cigarette-smoking businesswoman who was sharp and to the point. There was no room for silliness in her world, so I kept still and quiet while she talked to my mother about a work permit and a Coogan account. I remember thinking, *This is it. I got in the door.* I couldn't stop smiling. It was a dream come true.

Within a day, Barbara sent me on auditions. The first meeting she sent me on was for modeling. It's not that I really wanted to be a model; it was just the first direction Barbara sent me in. In the hierarchy of acting, I was at the bottom—I had no experience, no connections, and no training. I had to go for whatever was out there, and not be picky. That meant going on auditions that other girls rejected, like modeling underwear for catalogs or doing hand modeling for products or spending my Christmas break auditioning when everyone else was on vacation.

My parents never pushed me or told me to do these things. I wanted to be an actress, and this was my way to get in. I was willing to do anything to make that happen.

As a pre-teen, I traveled from Hicksville Station on the LIRR (Long Island Rail Road) to New York City two to three times a week, going on fittings and cattle calls. A cattle call was an audition, but for 30 to 40 girls who would simultaneously show up at the same time all to compete for the same job. We'd all wait an hour or so in the waiting room to be seen.

With modeling, it was short and simple. You showed your portfolio, tried on an outfit, and had a Polaroid (instant photo) taken. There was no callback for modeling. The clothes either fit or didn't fit, and that's how you got the job. What I didn't know at the time was that New York was the modeling capital of the world, and I was in for an education.

I learned many things from modeling, one of them being how to behave professionally, or as I like to call it, "professional etiquette." This included being punctual, waiting around patiently for hours until the photographer was ready to shoot, and standing perfectly still like a mannequin (even if my arms got tired) while a seamstress pinned and pulled while fitting my clothes. Sometimes I had to put on some really ugly outfits and not complain about it. *Glamour* is not the word that comes to mind.

But despite the uncomfortable aspects of the work, I learned essential knowledge about professional protocol, and I gained confidence working in the adult world. Modeling taught me self-discipline, stillness, punctuality, patience, and, ironically, how to smile naturally on cue. I learned this through trial and error while going out for jobs.

Luckily, I caught on quickly, and at 10 years old, I booked my first professional modeling gig. It was a print ad for a company propagating compulsive buying—scary, but true. I, of course, didn't realize the implications of the advertisement. In fact, I don't think I even knew what the client was "selling" until after the ad came out. The message certainly had an effect.

Regardless, doing the job was very exciting and made me feel proud to work at such a young age.

Another aspect about modeling that could not be ignored was the requirement to be slim. Even child models had to worry about weight. This comes from the idea that the body shouldn't distract from the clothes (and yes, it's all about selling clothes). Yet, being skinny was not in my genes.

I was born from German/Austrian stock and was not what you would call "naturally thin." I was more on the . . . healthy side, or what some might consider chubby. So my weight became a modeling issue.

Today, one might be open to discuss weight maintenance with a child for health reasons. But in the 70s, weight watching for a kid was not discussed at all. It wasn't taboo. It was more the idea that focusing on your body as a child was kind of narcissistic. Kids were to be kids, and they weren't to be worrying about their appearance in that way. If a child had some extra pounds, it was called *baby fat,* and people just hoped the kids would grow into it.

But at 10 years old, I was not growing into my baby fat. My body was changing from a child to a woman, and more weight was coming on.

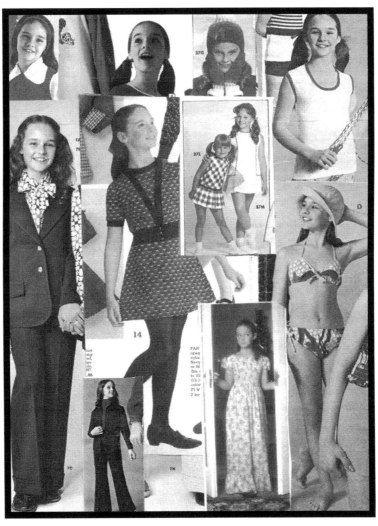

1970s catalog modeling

To make matters worse, my mom was an excellent cook.

She would make these delicious ethnic dishes like spatzel dumplings, goulash, Vienna schnitzel and one dish that was like hot vanilla pudding! Food was an interest we shared as a family.

Food brought us together at the beginning and end of the day. So how could I possibly model? I wasn't going to become anorexic or bulimic. That didn't seem like a solution to me, and frankly, I enjoyed food too much.

At 10 years old I was pre-boys, pre-body awareness, and pre-fitness craze, so I couldn't even count on external forces to help me lose weight. I had to take it on myself if I was going to be slim.

So I went to my mom and asked for her help in maintaining my weight. Going to her was important because, as a child, I couldn't do the shopping or make the meals. I needed someone to help me, not with motivation, but with pre-planning healthier meals instead.

Mom stopped making me two eggs every morning, and gave me egg whites instead. Brie sandwiches were a thing of the past—turkey or chicken sandwiches replaced those. I stopped asking for seconds at meals and ate celery and carrots sticks in the fridge instead. It was a team effort, and it worked.

Easy it was not. But it wasn't that difficult either, because I had my mom on my side. Mom understood how much my career meant to me, and she made adjustments to help me do it. But that choice was driven by my motivation. And my motivation was the standards of modeling.

Today we live in a more health-conscious society. Parents teach kids to take care of their bodies and to exercise daily, but when I was a kid in the 70s, if it had not been for modeling, I would have definitely gained unnecessary weight, and it would've followed me into adolescence and adulthood.

I also made up a *five-pound rule*. I never let myself get more than five pounds over weight. That meant if I went to a party and had some chocolate cake, I didn't go all crazy with the portions. I enjoyed the treat, and then I'd eat a salad at my next meal. I just tried to balance my diet and live a balanced life. I did not want to be food-obsessed either way.

So rather than choosing a life about just losing weight, I chose a life about weight maintenance. Which brings me to another point: The center of my happiness was not food. It was performing. So I spent more time pursing my interests rather than pursuing the refrigerator. I did ballet three times a week, went on auditions, and got involved in school activities. Having interests, other than eating, helped me stay in shape.

I quickly learned how to work with all kinds of adults, including those who were unprofessional or rude. In general, photographers and their assistants try to focus on the shot, and work quickly. They are not there to not coddle the talent. That was to be expected. Yet, sometimes adults would take their frustrations out on the kids even if the kids weren't doing anything wrong.

One notorious New York catalog photographer would yell at everybody, including his child models, throughout his shoots. My mother asked me if I wanted to stop working for him, but I told her no. Like any job, I could choose to quit, but being from New York, I prided myself on not backing down or being intimidated. So I refused to take it personally and I just let him rant. He was the one with the bad attitude, not me. I was not going to give up. Ironically, he hired me on a regular basis.

Modeling taught me a wide range of practical life lessons. I learned I could earn a living doing something I loved. It was a challenge going to a public middle school and having a professional career at the same time, but it was exciting and I could handle it. I loved the fast- paced energy and spontaneity mixed with the structure and self-discipline.

I learned how to organize myself and use my time wisely. More was expected of me, but all this made me feel grounded and competent.

I learned making a living wasn't easy. When I modeled for Macy's, JC Penney, Sears, and Bloomingdales, I would wear summer clothes in the winter, and winter clothes in the summer. This was especially taxing if the shoot was outdoors. I'd either be dripping sweat in the sun, wearing a parka in August, or freezing to the point of shaking, wearing a bikini in January, both with a smile on my face. It may sound abusive to do that to a child today, but back then it was the norm. I learned that sometimes I'd have to do things I didn't like in order to earn a living, but that didn't mean I had to give up pursuing my dream. Rather, I learned to toughen up and do my best. I showed myself I was a hard worker and persevering.

I quickly learned, however, that life wasn't going to give me a map to success. I had to chart that territory on my own. But first I had to figure out what *being successful* meant to me.

As I discovered, being successful was making a living as an actress, and having many different kinds of performing experiences. And I really do remember making that decision as a pre-teen.

After figuring that out, I had to find my path, and believe me, we each have our own unique paths to take. For me, I had no connections and no real professional guidance, so I knew I had to work my way up the ladder. I continually let people know what I wanted to do. I found people who understood me, and I sought their help, which was sometimes the hardest part if people didn't support my vision. But I kept putting it out there and eventually I connected with people who pushed me along.

In the end, I just went after what I wanted. Frankly, this is the part that separates the men and women from the boys and girls. I had to be brave to live the life I wanted, and I couldn't give up on myself. I had to be on my own side, and that meant not being a fair-weather friend to myself. I had to focus on doing good work. I always felt, deep down, that I had something worthwhile to share with the world, and that's what kept me on track, moving forward.

As a result, I was a very independent child. In middle school, when kids are usually trying to fit in, I didn't have that problem. I didn't struggle with peer pressure or approval because I had my interests to keep me busy and confident.

I think that if my parents had not listened to me or if they didn't support my vision during this crucial stage of development, I would have probably gone into depression or rebelled. But fortunately, they were open enough to be non-judgmental and to accept me for who I was and who I wanted to be. Their understanding was essential to my success.

Yet, as demanding as it was to be working as a child, I have many fun memories of modeling.

I flew to the Doral Hotel in Florida for a week to do a teen fashion shoot with a bunch of really nice girls. It was to introduce the midi length for young teens, and I remember actually feeling *cool* for the first time, that I was able to wear this fashion before anyone else got to wear it. We shot on boats, on the beach, at the hotel. It was really exciting, especially for a 12-year-old.

I also enjoyed being photographed for the book cover of *City Boy*, a Herman Wouk novel. They put me in clothes from the 40s and I got to acts as the character for the picture. Artists transformed the shot into an illustration for the book cover.

Right out of the gate, I developed a love for doing fashion shows and runway modeling. I did one show on a platform on the streets of New York. For those who know New York, you can imagine the traffic jam.

I also did a fashion show at the Waldorf Astoria hotel for fake fur coats. It was a very elegant experience, but I still skipped down the runway anyway in all my excitement.

I got to meet and work with a core group of young girls in the early 70s who also started their careers with modeling. Lisanne Falk (*Less Than Zero*), and Felice Schachter (*The Facts of Life, Zapped*) were a couple of the nicest friends I made during this time. In addition, one of these preteen girls was Brooke Shields. I met her and her mother on a bathing suit shoot.

Even then there was talk of Brooke's incredible beauty and anticipation of her huge career. She had either just shot, or was just about to shoot the film *Pretty Baby*, but you would never know she was doing something so impressive. In person, she was just this very sweet, slightly awkward, regular kid. She was not only humble and grounded, but the thing I liked most about her was that she gave pretty girls a good reputation. Meaning: Just because she was beautiful, didn't mean she had to be arrogant. She was funny, self-effacing and really nice. There was nothing elitist about Brooke. She was a hard worker and seemed to have the same kind of work ethics I had.

Brooke and I never competed for roles because I was slightly older, but she and her mother were always very nice to me whenever we saw each other. And while I never got to know her well, she surprisingly influenced my life in a big way.

A couple of years later, I acted as an extra in a film called *Endless Love,* which Brooke starred in. I had never been on a movie set before, but there I was, in a scene playing a punk rocker. Watching Brooke work was amazing. She was not only beautiful and elegant, but also very natural and humble. She even remembered me between shots, and let me take a photo of us together.

I remember leaving that job thinking I didn't need to be an actress anymore. Brooke embodied everything I wanted to be as a performer and I was happy for her. The odd thing was I felt at peace with it, not jealous. I thought, *Maybe I'm not meant to be an actress. Maybe there's something else I'm meant to do.*

But then it came to me: *There is room in the world for more than one person to attain their goal. Just because someone does what you want to do, doesn't mean you don't have your own gifts to offer.*

It was a turning point in me that Brooke unknowingly inspired.

Another aspect I had in common with Brooke was the closeness we each had with our moms. If you were to look for a single thread that links young actresses to their success, I would say that it was their mother's influence.

My mother wanted a better life for me and, therefore, not only helped me get an agent, drive me around, and generally support me, but she gave me her time and her attention. I guess in some cases, it might be pushy or controlling, but in my case, hanging out with my mom was part of the fun.

I loved traveling to the city with her, taking the train, subway, or rushing through the busy streets. It was an exciting adventure and it kept us close. My mom had a positive attitude, and she didn't care about the results. It didn't matter if I got the job. She just wanted to see me happy, and she enjoyed my life.

So I learned that *outcome* was not important, but that *process* was. I was very lucky to have my mom spending so much time with me. It wasn't easy for her to do. I will always be grateful for her.

Despite what most people might say about a modeling career, modeling had a positive effect on my life. It gave me the tools I needed to move forward in pursuing my dreams. And while success doesn't happen without the help and support of others, acting professionally taught me to be a self-starter. I didn't wait for others to make it happen.

Modeling was my first step in the big picture of becoming a professional actress. If you didn't like it at this point, you got out. But I loved it. I loved the demands, the spontaneity, and the adventure of being in the entertainment world.

Photo by Thomas Kriegsmann

Commercials

At 5 feet 2 inches, my modeling career was suddenly cut short and my commercial career began. It's funny how what you *can't* do guides you into what you *can* do.

Acting in commercials was a natural transition for me because I had an upbeat disposition and a lot of energy. I also now had enough practice taking direction from photographers and working in front of cameras to be sent out on calls.

Commercial auditions were one to four times a week, not including callbacks or fittings, and all of this took place in New York City. Now, at the age of 13, my mom would drop me off at the train station, where I'd ride into New York to meet my dad—who worked as a purchasing agent for New York Life. My dad and I would rush by bus, subway or on foot, to make the call on time.

The actual auditions took about five minutes apiece. But waiting to be called in could take as long as an hour. These people would see about 20 girls for one role, and then narrow it down to about five for callbacks a week later. If you got the job, you went for a wardrobe fitting. Within a couple days after that, you shot the commercial.

So *getting* a commercial meant traveling to the city at least four times within a two-week period for just one commercial. This doesn't include other commercial auditions that might come along. Auditioning, you could say, became extremely time-consuming. Yet, booking a commercial was a numbers game—the more you auditioned, the better your chances were to get a job.

I went out on every commercial possible to increase my chances. When other actors booked out for vacations, I made myself available. When other girls did not want to advertise toilet paper or deodorant, I did. When others stayed home with a cold, I went in sick with a smile. In addition, during this time, not every parent was willing or able to take their kids on auditions before the age of 18, after which the competition grew dramatically. Plus, by portraying someone younger than my age, my odds increased to work as well. By being strategic, I was able to increase my chances of success and, as a result, I booked a commercial about once a month.

My first commercial was for Weaver Fried Chicken. At the shoot, I could not, for the life of me, remember the name of the product, even though I was hired from the audition and the callback. We had a restaurant near my hometown called *Wetsons'*, and so, take after take I kept flubbing the line saying, "I love *Wetsons'*! It's delicious!" instead of saying "I love *Weaver*! It's delicious!"

Needless to say, the clients were not amused, and I was mortify-ably embarrassed. After that experience, my memory improved radically.

When I first started earning money through modeling, my parents put it into a savings account. When I got my first commercial check, I asked my dad to use the money for something special. I'd seen something I thought my mom would really enjoy. It was a new invention that would save her a ton of work. It was a clothes dryer. Not glamorous, but hardly anyone had one at home during the time because dryers were fairly expensive.

I bought one for her. I was so excited I could buy it with my own money. My mom loved it!

My parents put the rest of my residuals away for college. They had no aspirations to send me to college, but I did. I wanted to experience college life and become more educated. I knew at a young age I would not have been able to afford college had I not earned a living and paid for it myself. Indeed, the most rewarding aspect of doing commercials was that I earned my own living. That helped build my self-esteem and confidence, and it made me feel proud and happy. Ironically, pride and happiness is something money can't buy.

I also had my own working standards. I wanted to book an acting job once a month. Anything. Just something. It didn't matter if it was a hand-modeling job for a soap ad, an extra job in a commercial, or a speaking role in a film. If I didn't book, I re-examined what I was doing and tried to fix it. Was I trying too hard? Was I not doing it for myself? Was I not interpreting the material correctly? Was I putting myself out there enough? I always looked to myself first if work wasn't flowing.

Next, I committed 100 percent to every audition, whether I was right for the part or not. In other words, I didn't wait to book the job to give it my all. I committed to each audition right away as if I had the part. I would memorize the lines from the sides as well as from the rest of the script in the event the director should want to try another scene. This was important because I owned the character right away.

When I met with casting directors, I wasn't *trying out* for the part. I would simply *be* the part. Some roles I got, some roles I didn't get. Some parts I wanted. Some parts I didn't want. But this was how I rolled.

I also did not take *not getting the part* personally. I could never have acted for a living if I did. I didn't see *not getting* a part as rejection. To me, I saw it as, *I just wasn't what the director or producer had in mind.*

However, I did feel it was important to give a great read. If I wasn't right for one project, perhaps I was right for something else. A part that was right for me would come along eventually. This is not to say I wasn't disappointed if I didn't get the part I wanted. I just didn't let it affect my self-esteem. I let it go.

When I turned 16, I booked a popular geleatin commercial as the featured player. We shot from 3 p.m. to 3 a.m. on a sound stage in New York, and the last shot of the night was a close-up of me eating the gelatin and smiling. Everyone was pretty tired and wanted to get the shot done as fast a possible, and so I ate the green gelatin over and over again, not wanting to cause any problems.

Yet, at a certain point, I started feeling queasy and used the spit bag that I originally turned down. The experience taught me to ask for what I needed as an actress and, yes, never eat green gelatin again

I was chosen for a highly coveted commercial introducing the *Coke is it* campaign, which was one of the first one-minute commercials ever to be produced (up to that point, spots were typically as long as 30 seconds). It was a huge production, and was shot by film auteur Sidney Lumet's frequent cinematographer Andrzej Bartkowiak.

The concept was to show Coke as the inspiration behind a Broadway musical. They hired real Broadway actors for the spot. I was very surprised to find myself in the formula. I did sing and dance, but I was lucky enough to get a product shot. Years later, the commercial was exhibited at a Coca-Cola tribute in Las Vegas.

During this time, I got to work on commercials with many yet-to-be-discovered talents such as cool Matthew Modine (*Full Metal Jacket*), where I played a cheerleader and he played a football player, a Cheetos commercial that was a mini-musical starring the fabulous Jane Krakowski (*Ally McBeal, 30 Rock*) and I even got to go to Coney Island with beauty Lori Loughlin to shoot another Coke commercial.

Yet, not all the child actors moved on to film and television. Not every child can or wants to handle the lifestyle of being an actress/actor. As a result, there were only a handful of kids who stuck with it.

Week after week, I would see familiar faces at auditions. Even my best friend, Jeff Rhode (AKA Jeff Mitchell), who I helped get into commercials, did a Tic-Tac spot with awesome Ally Sheedy (*The Breakfast Club, WarGames*). At this point, whoever hung in there understood how to be professional and how to act.

And while the competition decreased, the level of competition that remained got much stiffer. I had to stand out in a different way.

Up until 1976, every commercial I went out for required straight hair. It was the fashion, I suppose. But it was also desired as a clean look that did not distract from the product. It was the look of the 70s kid, and if I wanted to work in commercials, I needed to conform.

I blow-dried my hair as straight as I could, until one day it was raining and I couldn't fight the humidity of the East Coast anymore. There was a last-minute audition for Trident Sugarless Mints, and I arrived with my huge mop of curly hair.

I remember thinking, *Why should I even bother going in for this? I look too messy. They're never going to pick me.*

Then, shockingly, I got a callback. More amazing than that, I booked the job! My hair, which was once perceived by the general public as frizzy, was now considered hip. This was a life-altering moment that even Sarah Jessica Parker could not deny. What was once a hindrance now became an asset.

So now curly hair was accepted. *Different* was *in*. And not only was I hired for the commercial, but also, when I was on set, I was selected out of a large group of kids to be featured in the spot. I got to sing the commercial jingle and dance.

I remember thinking, *I can't believe I was picked to do this with my wild hair.*

I had a great time working on the Trident spot, which turned out to be my breakout commercial. The ad ran on TV so much that people on the street in New York would recognize me. I was suddenly identifiable. From then on, I started going on auditions with curly hair.

Commercials taught me many things. I learned to focus, practice the economy of movement, keep repetitive actions fresh, improvise with other actors fluidly, take blocking and direction quickly, and, ironically, just be myself.

Commercial acting is not for everyone, but I enjoyed the discipline it took. It was one more skill I learned on my way to becoming an actress of all trades.

Photo by Thomas Kriegsmann

Teen Years 13 - 17: Theater and Soap Opera

Theater

I started doing plays in elementary school. My first role was in a production about safety. A boy, dressed as a policeman, helped me across the street. I remember feeling really nervous—or excited, depending on how you looked at it.

This was a big improvement from my preschool days, when my teacher noted I didn't like to pretend at all. I thought pretending was silly. I liked being real. Even as a young child, it was important for me to *be* the character, not *act* the character.

When I was in fifth grade, I got the role of Tuptim in *The King and I*. It was the first time I ever tried out for a singing role, and I felt very honored when I got the chance to sing a solo on stage. My voice shook a lot, but when it was all over, I felt great. I had so much fun that I wanted to do it again.

However, the middle school I later attended had no drama programs. That's when I started modeling. I had to wait until high school to do plays again.

Once I entered Plainview Old-Bethpage High, the first thing I did was join a Friday-night school group called Teen Club. In Teen Club, I learned acting games and improvisation. I played my first inanimate object: a lamp. I thought, *This is the stupidest thing I've ever done.* But everyone else in the class felt the same way. That was how we bonded—through laughter and embarrassment. And it became a great time.

Scholastically, I had to stay ahead of my schoolwork and keep my grades up in high school, not only for college, but also so my teachers would approve my work permit every six months. And I had to cover myself in case I had to miss school for work. It was very unconventional in the 70s to have a career as a child. Schools did not exactly know what to do with you when it came to missing classes. The only other actor who went to my high school was John Savage (*The Deer Hunter*), and he may have waited until after high school to pursue his career.

In order to stay in honor classes, I had to show my teachers that I was serious about my education, as I was about my career. Again, this was my call. I wanted to go to college and earn my grades. I didn't want to be treated special just because I acted.

The one thing I did want, however, was the freedom to pursue my career. It's almost as if, once I decided what I wanted to do, everything fell into place. Even when I had drama cadet rehearsals, the play director, Diane Misho, and the musical director, Ken Fries, knew I acted professionally and still allowed me in our school productions because they knew I wouldn't let them down. It just worked out. Ironically, at 15, I learned part of being a real actress was not being flaky.

I auditioned for several school productions and, in 9th grade, was cast as Brigitta in *The Sound of Music*. It was very exciting because I got to act with older kids and actually have a speaking part.

In 10th grade, I played Sarah Brown in *Guys and Dolls*, which was a life-altering experience for me. Not only did I make some very close friends, but I also fell in love for the first time. It was real, deep, and true love. Sadly, I had to break up with the boy in order to pursue my career. It was very painful for both of us. He never left my mind, however, as he was the inspiration behind my final scene in the film *The Last American Virgin*.

Decades later, my daughter played the same role as I did for her 8th grade school production of *Guys and Dolls*. It was the greatest case of déjà vu I've ever experienced.

In 11th grade, I performed as Hope Harcourt in *Anything Goes*, which had a great cast. And in 12th grade, I was chosen to play the role of Rosemary Pilkington in *How to Succeed in Business Without Even Trying*, playing opposite my closest friend, Jeff .

High school plays taught me about voice projection, working with other actors, and staying in the moment even if I made a mistake. Personally, I think mistakes—or at least the possibility of making mistakes—are what make theater so exciting. There are those golden moments that remind the audience—and the cast—that anything can happen at any time.

I also loved acting in high school musicals because one usually got to play adult characters. It was like trying on Mom's high heels as a little girl. You got to see life from a different perspective.

But the best part about doing a high school musical was that you bonded with other cast members. I made a lot of good friends through high school drama, some of whom I am still friends with today.

Because singing was such a strong passion of mine, I took private singing lessons from an opera singer and teacher named Theresa Arrigo, joined the school choir, and got into madrigals between ages 13 and 16. I participated in New York State Music Association competitions singing operatic and classical pieces, and learned about breath control, phrasing, harmonies, projection, placement, and creative expression.

I loved singing so much that I would spend hours in the basement at my piano writing my own songs and recording them onto my 8-track reel-to-reel player. I just loved music.

Yet, because I did not have a strong singing voice, I did not gravitate toward a musical theater career. And, even though I had years of dance training, I did not have the body type to compete with true professional dancers. So I kept my focus on acting.

Dressed as Rosemary Pilkington for my 12th grade musical,
How to Succeed in Business Without Really Trying (1980)

During these years, I did a lot of voice-over work for radio. I learned about articulating, phrasing, speech patterns, voice lilt, rhythm, music in the voice, time restraints, booth etiquette, creating characters through attitudes, and simply how to use a microphone.

I found voice-over work to be invaluable to my acting. When I isolated my acting to my voice, I automatically imagined the kind of person who was speaking, and learned that the voice was the soul of the character. It's what makes the character real and recognizable. Over the years, people have approached me and said, "Your voice is the same as it was in the movie . . ." or "I totally recognize your voice."

I never thought I had an unusual voice, but I do have a high voice, which worked for playing young characters. The fun part, as I got older, was being able to use my lower register as well. It gave me more range in the kind of roles I could play.

When I was 15, director Michael Kahn cast me in my first professional play in the role of JoBeth Williams'(*Poltergeist, The Big Chill*) daughter, Caroline Kirby, in *The Happy Journey from Camden to Trenton*. I got to take a month off from school, and I lived in an apartment with my mom in Princeton, New Jersey.

I was to perform at the McCarter Theater, which was this enormous theater, with only a 6-person cast. Ironically, this enriching experience caused me to go down from honors English to regular English for missing a month of school.

The rewards, however, far outweighed the consequences. Theater taught me stamina, how to take my time with dialogue, how to use my body to create a stage picture and to pace myself, and how to reserve my energy to make it through the entire performance.

I really enjoyed doing plays. But because I did not come from a family that promoted theater, and because I watched so much television, I tended to gravitate toward performing in film and TV. That made performing in plays even more of a privilege when I got the chance to do them.

What theater didn't teach me was to be subtle. Everything in school plays was about being bigger and more animated. When I started going on film and television auditions, I had to tone it way down. Some casting directors tried to get me to tone it down by telling me to "just be myself." That typically didn't work. I was naturally a more animated person, and being myself was still too colorful for some.

I had to figure out a way to bring out the real me, and that's when I learned how powerful words can be. I had to find a word that worked for me that got the results casting directors and others wanted.

After a bit of experimenting, I found that the word *nondescript* worked for me. When I thought of being nondescript, I relaxed and pulled way back. You couldn't tell the difference between my conversations in a waiting room and my auditions.

It took a long time for me to trust that less is more, but I got my affirmations when I started booking jobs.

Photo by Dan Nelken

Soap Opera

How did I get my big break?

My biggest acting break of the 70s didn't come from a single job, director, or producer. It actually came from another actress—Brooke Shields.

Brooke changed the face of acting. Her role in *Pretty Baby* had a huge impact on how preteens were seen in film. In the 70s, girls were cast as tough tomboys, like Jodie Foster (*Alice Doesn't Live Here Anymore, Taxi Driver*) or Tatum O'Neal (*The Bad News Bears*) when they were kids.

In the 80s, a sexual revolution occurred that allowed girls to be seen as feminine and sexy. When this change took place, my success was directly affected.

The 80s allowed the fantasy of the young teen to be possible. Along with this allure, came the look—strong eyebrows. Strong eyebrows were suddenly sexy and the new craze. It was as if casting directors wanted Brooke Shields look-alikes, and whoever fit that description got the part.

But that didn't only apply to me. Other actresses with strong eyebrows also benefited, including Heather Langenkamp, Alyssa Milano, Claudia Wells, Alexandra Paul, Catherine Mary Stewart, Betsy Russell, Jami Gertz and Kristian Alfonso, to name a few.

The door was open, but that didn't mean success was guaranteed. Before I walked through, I wanted to make sure I knew what I was doing.

I decided to meet with an acting coach. I took a couple of private acting lessons, but it didn't feel right. I don't think I was ready to take in all the information. It put me too much in my head and not enough in the moment.

So I went back to acting with my instincts, connecting to situations with my heart, and watching others actors.

I studied actors/actresses on TV—with the sound off. I'd watch their body language and expressions, and I'd ask myself, "Do I really believe them?" "Are they sincere?" "What are they

doing or not doing that makes me believe they are these characters?" And the big question: "What makes one person more captivating than another?"

I discovered that my main acting education came from studying actors I believed were real or funny. Dramatic actresses/actors who influenced me the most were Robert De Niro, Meryl Streep, and Jack Nicholson, while comedic idols were Carol Burnett, Marlo Thomas, Lucille Ball, and Woody Allen.

Marilyn Monroe, Sophia Loren, and Elizabeth Taylor were also great inspirations. These women from an earlier era had an allure that I could relate to and a mature sexuality I wanted to bring out in my own acting. Although, I did not try to mimic these actresses, it was through their work that I found I had something special to say in my work.

In order for an actor/actress to stand out, I felt you had to have a voice, as in, I know what standing up against adversity is, or, I know what being a victim is, or, I know what being funny is.

What you have to say must be real and sincere, and it must come from you. It is the gift of information you share with the world, and it will make your work unforgettable. For me, I knew what love and sexuality were. And I was willing and able to show it off in my performances.

And then it happened.

When I turned 17, I was cast to play Lois Middleton, a recurring role on the soap opera *As The World Turns*. Mind you, I was still pretty animated. But here it worked for the medium.

I was the teen troublemaker, always trying to wrangle my friend Betsy into mischief. I played this role for six months. I had a blast playing a character that was so different from me in real life. I got a really good acting workout as well.

I learned to handle set pressure, memorize huge amounts of dialogue, and bring myself to tears in two takes—max. Although soap operas tend to have a notorious reputation for creating bad acting habits, acting on a soap has its benefits—it's the closest an actor can get to a 9-to-5 job, next to a series regular.

Soap opera actors must keep up with the fast pace, memorize dialogue quickly, and go with the flow. We shot hour-long shows in one day. That meant that if I was in the show three days in a row, I worked three days in a row. That also meant I got paid very well.

In 1979, I think I made about $500 per episode. In my junior year of high school, I would leave school early, travel to the city, go to the studio to shoot my scene, and return late that night to go to school the next day. In the instances where I worked three days in a row, I would perform this daily grind for three days straight. I was crazy busy, but I loved it. It was kind of like the TV show *Hannah Montana*; I had the best of both worlds.

My character, Lois Middleton, was nothing like me. She was into dating lots of boys, drugging, and drinking. At 17, in real life, I was kind of naïve about such things, although, I did have a boyfriend.

Ironically, the actress, Susan Davidson, who played the sheltered role of Betsy Stewart, later played by Meg Ryan (*When Harry Met Sally*), in reality was very worldly and experienced.

When the director yelled cut, I would be so nervous, asking, "Was that okay?" while Betsy would just leave the set without saying a word.

Betsy was a seasoned pro with a guaranteed contract. I did not have that luxury. But doing *As the World Turns* prepared me for the demands of acting in the big time, and that made me feel I could make a living as a working actress.

No matter how busy I was with my career, I still had time to have a teenage life. Kids in school knew I acted, but they didn't treat me any different. That's not to say everyone may have liked me, but the people at my high school were grounded.

I had a wide range of friends in different groups, and I never felt pressured to be in a clique. I think that's because I found out what I wanted to do early in my life, and I had already started pursuing it. That's what I loved most about going to high school—I could be myself.

I had friends, best friends, and boyfriends. I went to the mall, went to the beach, and went bowling. I ice-skated, skied, played mini-golf, took hikes. I went to proms and fell in love. I learned a lot about life in high school. And one of the things I learned was that not all knowledge comes from books. Life has much to give, too.

Part of living life was deciding whether to go to college or not. I was a solid honors B+ student—not the best grades for college. And my SAT scores weren't that great either. However, I did have an impressive acting reel, which I think showed promise as a high achiever.

I really wanted to go to college and learn. More truthfully, I wanted to know what everyone was talking about. Going to college was as common as watching television. The path of higher education may not have been essential as an actress, but I knew I needed to learn as much as possible about the world in a bigger way. Since no one in my family had gone to college, I had no expectations except that it would be an adventure.

I applied to three schools—Princeton (because I had seen it when I did the play at the McCarter Theater), UCLA (because it was in Los Angeles where the entertainment business thrived), and NYU (because it was local and I could continue my acting auditions at the same time).

I didn't get into Princeton. But UCLA and NYU accepted me. I chose to go to NYU. I was excited about living in the city. I would still be able to visit my family on the weekends.

Here's the bizarre part: I wanted to study something I couldn't possibly learn on my own. Since I was paying for it, I wanted to choose something that really interested me. Would you believe it? Biochemistry really interested me. I was always fascinated with science, and somewhere in the back of my mind I wanted to find a cure for cancer. Crazy, maybe, but I do think big.

I chose biochemistry as my major and really got into it. But I had no intentions of giving up on acting. My plan was to go to school and audition just as I had done in high school. I felt that the more education I had, the more it grounded me in the roles I played. And if I ever I had to play a scientist, well . . . I'd know what I was talking about.

During the same time, a personal assistant came to work for Barbara Jarrett named Suzie Moore. Suzie was a talented actress as well, had lots of energy, and spoke with a charming Southern dialect. She was supportive and caring to all her clients, but for some reason, she took a special interest in me. We really bonded, and as a result she boosted my career. She believed in me.

This was important because you can't toot your own horn. To make it in the entertainment business you need to find someone you can trust who *gets* you and then back you. You need a teammate.

She submitted me for projects that required an 18-year-old to play younger, which was common practice in the business because much of the work restrictions placed on children are for under-18 performers. Of course, personally, at 18, I would have preferred to look older. I wanted to be seen as an adult. But I wanted to work more, so I used my young looks to my advantage.

That's when I turned into a real adult. In order to make a living as an actress, I needed to think like an adult. My short height made me look younger than a lot of other girls, and it made my male co-stars look taller.

Beginning in 1980, with the help of my manager, Suzie Moore, and my new, theatrical agents, the Gage Group, (run by the incredibly considerate Martin Gage who actually bought me a cake to celebrate joining his agency), I began going out for film and television roles.

OVER 18

Photo by Joseph D'Allessio

Angel or Siren?

In the early 80s, I was either cast as the angelic ingénue or as the searing siren. Both roles are classic female archetypes that can be seen throughout cinema history.

The good girl—or the ingénue—was the young, innocent female who was usually a victim of circumstance. I was cast as the ingénue because I looked and acted very young and naive. I was also over 18. This allowed me to travel alone, work longer hours, and relieve production from having to deal with work restrictions for minors.

Photo by Doyle Gray

But it was not just for practical reasons that I got these parts. Since I was raised with European sensibilities, I understood old-fashioned gender dynamics, and was able to play very vulnerable girls. Such was the case in playing Karen in *The Last American Virgin*. With my angelic curls, pale skin, and my small frame, I looked the part. But I still had to play it as soft and vulnerable as possible.

I modeled the character after a girl in a film from Israel called *Lemon Popsicle*. The girl was the object of desire—an object of beauty—seen but not heard, feminine, passive, and not a real American 80s girl at all. Personally, at the time, I was quite opposite of the character. I was assertive, traveling on my own, paying my expenses, and making a good living.

But I did understand the plight of a passive girl. Even though I was assertive in going after a career, personally I was timid in many ways. I wasn't confident in communicating verbally. I relied heavily on eye contact and gestures. As a result, I was easily vulnerable to men. Because of this, I could totally relate to Karen. She was like prey—a bunny or a fawn. She was the kind of girl who wouldn't know what danger was until it was too late.

Photo by Manny Rodriguez

My European sensibilities certainly helped me play the ultimate ingénue. But they also enabled me do nudity in the film. I showed, in body and voice, a passive girl's experience of life in the early 80s, for better or for worse.

Personally, I wanted the audience to see that, even with all the freedoms women have in expressing their 80s independence (such as having sex more casually, or the ability to have an abortion), it doesn't change the fact that life still isn't easy for girls, and they can still make bad decisions. Those who have seen the end of *Last American Virgin* know what I mean. Playing the ingénue, I taught big life lessons. Perhaps that is why these roles are so memorable. The ingénue teaches young girls to wake up.

The ingénue is such a revered, deep-seeded female archetype that there is often a perverse desire to taint her image. The result of destroying her innocence takes the form of a different archetype: the siren.

The siren is the seductress—the predator. She is like a cat or tiger. She is completely in control, calculating, and manipulative (and very fun to play!). She is associated with being the bad girl in a story, and usually played using great sexuality to gain power.

I was able to play these women with complete ease because I was comfortable with my own sexuality. Whenever I played a siren, I expressed my feminine character using sultry, smooth movements, or behaving coquettishly. This was distinctly different from the typical American teen.

American teens in 80s films expressed their sexuality through sweet awkwardness, and made a strong impression, such as Molly Ringwald's character did in *Sixteen Candles*, or Deborah Foreman's character did in *Valley Girl*.

Teens were written to be uncomfortable with their bodies and romance. This was the American style of the "good girl". If a teen was confident with her sexuality, then audiences assumed she had to be the trouble-maker, such as Lea Thompson's frisky character in *Back to the Future* or Rebecca DeMorney seductive role in *Risky Business*.

The siren role was a temptress. Yet, an actress playing the same role as *adult* in the 80s had a completely different effect on moviegoers. A woman character who was confident about her own femininity in the 80s was heroic, like Melanie Griffith in *Working Girl* or Jennifer Beals in *Flashdance*. The American style of *adult* female sexuality was direct and free-spirited.

I was able to play the classic sultry siren, as seen in the movie of the week *Summer Girl* because, again, I had grown up with a European influence. Additionally, I was not afraid to explore my own sensuality. I communicated more with my body and eyes than I did with words, and I would slow down the pace of a scene to express the power of my character. I allowed my own personal intensity to come out in scenes, which kept it real and captivating.

Another character I played that flipped into siren was Patricia Montelli in *Amityville II: The Possession*. Patricia starts out as a naïve ingénue, and ends up as a devilish seductress seducing a priest.

While the film deals with incest, what is truly upsetting is that no *real* girl from the 80s would have acted so passive. Patricia Montelli was based on an old-fashioned stereotypical archetype that I brought to life playing her with delicacy and conviction. Perhaps, this is why people find my character and the story so disturbing.

I portrayed both archetypes in the film *Second Time Lucky*. This was the story of Adam and Eve reincarnated throughout history.

The character Eve was the original ingénue, and, of course, once seduced by the snake to consume the forbidden apple of knowledge, she becomes the seductress. While I loved playing the role as an actress, I felt this was definitely not how 80s women behaved, and it made the film seem rather dated. It was more of a male fantasy with stereotypical gender roles than it was based in reality.

Women in the 80s didn't want to be perceived as angels or sirens. They didn't want to be seen as objects. American women wanted to be seen as strong, smart, and self-sufficient. They wanted to make their own life choices rather than be passive victims of circumstances. Yet, I can't blame men for wanting to watch women being soft and seductive on screen, especially if it was not necessarily available in 80s reality. Perhaps this is why sexuality on screen is so powerful and captivating.

Regardless of the role I portrayed on screen, I had to be a very patient, determined, and self-motivated actress in real life to compete in the entertainment industry.

My role as an 80s babe changed over the years. In the early part of the decade, I played more of the "male fantasy" roles, acting as the passive, innocent objects of desire. Yet, by the mid 80s, I got to play more independent, intelligent, and self-assured characters, becoming more of a female role model.

It wasn't until the mid 1980s that I finally got the chance to play someone who would later become a female role model. The French exchange student Monique Junet in *Better Off Dead* wasn't the ingénue or the siren. She was ironically more American in attitude than French, a spunky-spirited girl, and a role that was closest to my true personality.

Savage had written Monique as an endearing character who not only had a firm grip on life, but also an attractive quality because she was smart, funny, and brave. She did not have to be a seductive French sexpot to win the heart of the character played by John Cusack, nor did she have to be a passive waif needing to be saved. Monique took on a contemporary American approach to femininity by turning her oddity into charm.

In the 80s film *Some Kind of Wonderful*, Mary Stuart Masterson's teen character dressed as a boy and was somewhat tomboyish. But Monique took this one step further. Because she was French, the audience could accept her as being strong and feminine. Even the clothes Monique wore showed a new confidence. She didn't need to show off her body to be liked. You just had to get to know her. And once you did, the character's confidence, passion, and heart made you fall in love.

That character sent a big message to teens. This underground, word-of-mouth film said that a teen girl who was different could also be attractive. Monique contributed to breaking the mold of the 80s female teen in film. But where did most girls model their identity at the time? Television. Girls saw a mainstream image of what the typical American 80s teen should be like on T.V.

80s Television
1980-1989

Photo by Joseph D'Allessio

Too Good To Be True

As an actress, I portrayed the typical 80s teen, yet my personal goal wasn't to become famous, rich, or win awards. I wanted to experience different arenas of entertainment—commercials, voice-over, theater, film, TV, music videos, musicals, sit-coms, soaps . . . I wanted to try them all.

It's kind of like my philosophy on dating. When I was single, I wanted to go out with different types of guys to get some perspective. That takes a little time, and you may not know what you want out of the relationship at first, so you keep dating until, eventually, you find the right person.

In regard to acting, what came clear was my love of being creative. I enjoyed being an actress because it gave me a chance to use my imagination. When I was offered television roles, I thought, great, something completely different. This was the adventure I was looking for.

Too Good to Be True (1982) with handsome actor John Stockwell

I had two films under my belt, but I was longing for a more wholesome exposure.

ABC was interested in me for a new television pilot called *Too Good to Be True*. Reid Shelton (Daddy Warbucks from the Broadway show *Annie*) and Diana Muldaur (*L.A.Law*) were the stars.

I was to play Cassie, an attractive, grounded girl who lived in a co-ed boarding school. Cassie was the main love interest who, of course, plays hard to get. It was a progressive American female character, and a good role model for girls. I was very happy to be given the part.

I learned that working on a sitcom was similar to working on a play. We'd start with a table read on Monday, where we broke down the script with the cast. On Tuesday, Wednesday, and Thursday, we got script revisions, blocked out the scenes, and went for wardrobe fittings. On Friday, we'd perform in front of a live audience for the cameras.

On that pilot, I learned about timing, holding a beat for the laugh, keeping my energy up, and how to deliver a comedic punch line. I also became close with other members of the cast, including wonderful Moosie Drier, (Kids Incorporated, Laugh-In), handsome John Stockwell, (Top Gun, My Science Project) a very cool guy with a big personality, and Brian Backer (*Fast Times at Ridgemont High and Tony award winner*), who I had previously met working on a musical Coke commercial back in the 70s! Brian had this wonderful Woody Allen charm that always put a smile on my face.

Because I was flown in from New York, ABC put me up at the Hilton on Avenue of the Stars in Century City, which was connected underground to the ABC studio. It was very posh. And exciting to say the least.

I flew both my parents out from New York for the taping and they were really surprised when a limo picked them up from the airport. I paid for the limo and the hotel on Avenue of the Stars, and they couldn't believe it. At 20, I was able to treat them! It was really a gift for all of us.

When the show finally went up in front of the live audience, I learned a few more things. The audience responds to every moment, whether we shoot the scene three times or if we were in between scenes changing sets or if someone flubbed a line. It was like theater with behind-the-scenes in front of the scene. The audience saw everything that was going on—the crew, the sets, the cameras, the make-up. We actors and actresses had to stay focused on what we were doing and not get distracted.

Doing a sitcom reminds me of when basketball players are at the free throw line and the crowd is going crazy. You've got to relax and stay connected to what you are doing otherwise you'll miss the shot.

The pilot for *Too Good to be True* aired a few months later. Unfortunately, it did not get a picked up as a series. Yet, my work did not go unnoticed. ABC had another project in mind for me, and this time I was to be the lead.

Deadly Lessons

At the age of 20, ABC cast me in the lead role for a movie made for television, or as it was called then, Movie of the Week (MOW). It was called *Deadly Lessons,* originally called *The Girls from Stalkwater High.* I was to work with 1950s icon Donna Reed (*The Donna Reed Show*) and Larry Wilcox (*CHiPs*) on location in Los Angeles.

The story was about a young country girl entering a rich prep school, where a series of mysterious murders were taking place. One by one, girls were being murdered, except for my character, Stephanie, who ultimately uncovers the murderer's identity. I played my character as innocently as possible because I was the outsider. This was true in real life as well.

While I was flown in from New York, most of the other actresses playing students in the movie were already in Los Angeles. Some very exceptional actresses in the movie included wholesomely intense Ally Sheedy (*Breakfast Club, WarGames*) and the gifted Nancy Cartwright (*Simpsons*).

I had auditioned for the part in L.A. and, shortly after my flight back to New York to start the fall semester at NYU, I got a call saying I got the role. I jumped right back on a plane to California. I never imagined I was going to get the part because it was the lead, and I wasn't a name, so I just moved on with my life and returned to school. I was shocked when the network said they wanted me. And they wanted me right away because I had to begin horseback riding lessons for the part.

How fun was that! Horseback riding lessons, and a lead!

I had very little experience riding horses, but wasn't afraid of them, and loved animals. I was certainly not born to ride. However, I picked up trotting quickly. Luckily, my character was not supposed to be good at riding English style, so my skill level fit my character. What I did need to be really good at was screaming and crying. But since I had done a lot of that during *Amityville II*, I did at least feel prepared for that ride.

While shooting, I lived in the infamous Oakwood Garden Apartments in Burbank, a popular spot for actors and actresses to stay when visiting L.A. And even though I could drive, I was not able to rent a car until I was 21. Someone picked me up and drove me to the set or to the shooting location every day for a month.

When I met with the rest of the cast, it was a little awkward—just like it was for my character in the movie. *Who was this unknown girl from New York playing the lead?* the other actors must've thought. I mean, even I was surprised. Everyone was super nice, but it took a beat to warm up to the other girls.

Ally Sheedy was very nice to me and I feel fortunate to have worked with her. She was already on her way to becoming a huge success. I think she had just finished *War Games,* and had a lot going on.

Donna Reed was very genteel and professional, but our scenes were limited together.

Larry Wilcox stayed more to himself, most likely because of his character.

I spent most of my time hanging out with fellow students Nancy Cartwright (*Simpsons*) and Deena Freeman (*Too Close for Comfort*), who were both really friendly, unpretentious and very funny. We would joke around between scenes and even stayed friends after the job ended. Bill Paxton (*Titanic, Big Love*), who played my boyfriend in the movie, was very easy to work with. He was the kind of actor who would surprise you with every take and made doing our scenes fun. He was also sweet and genuine. I felt we had good chemistry together on screen – and off. We dated in real life afterward.

All in all, the cast bonded in the end, and I have many fond memories of the shoot.

Deadly Lessons was an important step in my career because it gave me a TVQ, which is the rating of an actor's performance based on the amount of viewers. Because the show got such good ratings, another network sought me out soon after. This time, surprisingly, they wanted me for a seductive role.

Summer Girl

At 21, CBS hired me to do an MOW called *Summer Girl*. AJ Carothers adapted Caroline Crane's novel, and Roberta Haynes and Edgar Lansbury produced. The part of Cinni became available after Diane Lane turned it down, for reasons I don't know. Such was my luck.

I went for several callbacks and finally got the chance to read for the network. I remember their concern that my name was not big enough, and that I was a little on the . . . healthy side. But after I wowed them with my reading, they realized they found their Summer Girl.

The story was about a frumpy babysitter who was hired to watch a couple of kids during the family's trip to Hawaii. The babysitter turns out to be a schizophrenic sociopath who seduces the husband, drugs the mother, kidnaps the kids, and pushes her ex-boyfriend off a cliff. You know—reality.

My character was very evil and very sexy. This was such a fun role to play because I got be creative. I based my split personalities on a bunch of different people I knew, and created different mannerisms and cadences for each persona. I was all ready for the part. But I had to tell one lie to get the job.

I told the network I was an excellent swimmer and extremely comfortable in the water. This, of course, was far from the truth. When I was 8 years old, I had tubes in my ears for a year and was not allowed to go swimming during that time. Because of this, I'd mildly panic in the water, looking more like a drowning cat than a hot babe. But I figured if I got the part, I'd deal with it then.

Myself, and awesome actors Barry Bostwick & Kim Darby

Well, surprise, I got the part! Now what do I do? I raced to a swimming instructor, who helped me go under water without freaking out. In one day I was able to go under water and be relaxed. I just kept visualizing my character in the water, not giving a (beep), and I was committed to play the part realistically.

Producer Roberta Haynes was instrumental in getting *Summer Girl* made. Roberta started her career as a stunning actress in the 50's (*Return to Paradise, Point Blank*) and got into producing to support projects for women. She and I became good friends. She knew how difficult it was to get a respectable role as an actress, and she worked very hard to make sure the entire cast was happy.

In February, Barry Bostwick (*The Rocky Horror Picture Show*), Kim Darby (*True Grit*) and who I would work again with in *Better Off Dead,* and I were flown to Oahu. to start shooting. The weather was breathtaking, but it was also Portuguese Man O' War jellyfish season, so we had to watch out that we didn't get stung in the water.

Lucky me, I had to wear all these revealing bathing suits, which I thought were pretty funny because there was no way a person could really swim in any of them. It took about a month to finish the movie, and we shot at a private home as well as the beach where they shot *From Here to Eternity*.

I loved playing Cinni because there were so many levels to the character. She was manipulative, seductive, callous, and just plain evil. Of all the different personalities I gave her, the one I thought was most challenging was that of indifference. *Not caring* is not me. It was the most opposite quality I had. I really had to visualize that type of person in order to capture the quality realistically. I had no acting coach or teacher to guide me. I was on my own and trusted my creative instincts.

I remember I did not want to play the character crazy, but rather totally entitled, which is what I think made her so scary.

Kim Darby was very sweet and supportive to me as an actress. She was so endearing in the film, I felt bad taking over her family. Luckily the authorities eventually picked up my character, so it all worked in the end.

David Faustino (*Married with Children*) and Laura Jacoby (*Uncle Buck*) were adorable and very professional kids. We all had a blast working together.

Working with Hunt Block (*Guiding Light*), who played my boyfriend, was like doing a scene with an Abercrombie fantasy model that can act. He was so sweet and just gorgeous, and all my scenes with him involved him fawning over me, and me being disinterested in him. I can't tell you how difficult it was to do that.

But I didn't mix business with pleasure because I didn't want to ruin the chemistry of the scene. I had to restrain myself through the whole project. Finally, when the shoot was over, he asked me out. I couldn't believe it! So, of course I said yes, and then fawned over him!

Barry Bostwick, who played the father in the family, was so much fun to work with. Not only is he extremely handsome with such a beautiful voice, but he also has such an easy-going disposition, and he's an extremely creative performer. I'll never forget him telling me that he had played so many different kinds of roles that it made it difficult for casting directors to define him as an actor. He was unique as well, so I always felt we were kindred spirits. To this day, I think he is a very special person who made everyone on the set feel happy and relaxed.

One of my closest high school friends who became a psychologist told me a pregnant client came to her one day complaining about this MOW called "Summer something," which made her afraid to hire a babysitter. My friend calmly told her it was just a role I played, and that in real life I was probably a really nice person. I felt terrible. I couldn't believe my acting was that believable!

My performance earned me a submission by the production company for an Emmy that year. But unfortunately, it wasn't selected.

I finished *Summer Girl*, worked back-to-back on three other projects, and was pretty exhausted. Yet, I still had to pull myself together for one more amazing work opportunity, and one of the most traumatic adventures of my life.

The Turning Point

Amadeus

Right after completing *Summer Girl* in Hawaii, I returned to L.A. and immediately found out that I had to fly to New York to audition for the role of Constanze, Mozart's wife, in the film *Amadeus*. The producers were in mid-production when their original choice for the lead, Meg Tilly, broke her leg. They needed to recast the role and were looking at every petite dark-haired girl they could find.

Well-known and cool casting director, Bonnie Timmerman, knew me from auditioning for other projects in New York. She requested me specifically.

The amazing part about this audition was when I was flying to Los Angeles to shoot *Summer Girl,* I sat next to a gentleman who was reading the *Amadeus* script. I asked him if he was an actor, and we got into conversation. He said that he had just finished shooting a film called *Scarface* and was on his way to play a role in a film about Mozart's life. He then looked at me and told me there was a role in the script that I would have been perfect for, but it had already been cast. This actor turned out to be F. Murray Abraham, who later won an Oscar for his role as Salieri in the film. It was sheer coincidence that I was called into the audition six months later.

The first audition was at the Hampshire Hotel in New York. The casting director put me on videotape. From that taped audition I got to meet director Milos Forman (*One Flew Over the Cuckoo's Nest*) the next day at the call back. I did not know whom he was or that he was legendary, so I was very relaxed. He had me do a few more scenes, and when we were finished he told me they were going to fly me and another actress to Prague, Czechoslovakia, in the next few days and make the decision there. It was that fast.

Because they were in the middle of filming, whoever got the role would stay, and the other would return to America. At 21 years old, although I felt very capable of traveling by myself, this was the most high-pressured situation I had ever been in. I had to remain calm and cool, even though I was incredibly excited.

The following Tuesday I was on a plane to Prague with the producer, Saul Zaentz (*The English Patient*), and the other actress. The other actress turned out to be talented Elizabeth Berridge, who I had actually worked with on *As The World Turns* in a party scene, and who had competed for the role in *Amityville II*, which I eventually got. We were both petite brunettes with sexual allure, but we had very different energy and style. I was always surprised when we would go up for the same roles because we were so different. Yet, here we were again, going up for the same role. Who would get it this time?

It was a rather awkward flight for the three of us, especially since I heard Saul favored Elizabeth. After a small connecting flight from Germany to Czechoslovakia, we finally made it to Prague. We were put up at one of the nicest hotels in the city, but had little time to sightsee.

The minute we got off the plane, we went to be fitted for costumes and wigs. The next day, Elizabeth and I would screen test with every scene in the film. I remember being in my hotel room that night just trying to ground myself and relax. Frankly, the auditioning part didn't worry me. I knew my lines and planned to just have fun and be in the moment. I knew this was a once in a lifetime opportunity, and I was going to enjoy the experience.

It was the competitive vibe that got me. It was quiet, intense, and very stressful. There was a lot of tension in the air, though nothing bad was ever said. The next day I screen-tested all day, and I felt good about my work. Elizabeth tested after me, and finally the pressure was over. Elizabeth and I went to dinner together, both relieved filming was over, and we admitted our true feelings about the whole situation to each other.

She had done a lot of acting training in New York and had even been in class with Tom Hulce (who played Mozart in *Amadeus*). I, on the other hand, had little to no training, but had a lot of work experience. We were just starting to relax when the director (Milos) came over and said we had to do the whole thing over again. It seems Elizabeth's test had some problems, so they needed to have us act out every scene in the entire movie one more time.

The $24 lettuce leaf I had just been eating made me full. The tension between us resumed, and we retreated from our friendly conversation. I went back to my room to rest and regroup for the next day.

It is so amazing that the most difficult part of being a professional actress isn't the acting; it's staying in a good head, remaining focused, and being relaxed. The next day we did all the scenes again, and again I felt good about my work. I did my best and felt confident.

At the end of the day, Milos sat us both down and said, "Diane, we made a decision. We have to give the part to Elizabeth. She has the right look."

Wow.

Whether he told me the truth or not, I don't know, but his response took me by surprise. I swallowed hard and took a beat to digest it. I had prepared for either decision, but I hadn't expected that. I responded with, "Whatever is best for the film is most important, but if possible, could I please have a copy of my screen test for me to remember this incredible experience?"

Milos said very sweetly he would see what he could do.

Elizabeth and I hugged, and I went back to my room to pack. I was shocked, shaken, and exhausted. I came so close, but it wasn't meant to be. As I flew back alone on the plane, I remember feeling disappointed, but I also felt a sense of relief. Elizabeth was going to do a great job. I was too tired. I needed a break.

Six months later, Saul Zaentz brought me back my test, and I will always be grateful to him for it. If I had gotten *Amadeus*, my life would have taken a very different turn. I would never have done the film *Better Off Dead,* met my great husband, or had my two incredible kids. What one might consider a loss was definitely a blessing in disguise.

Episodic Television

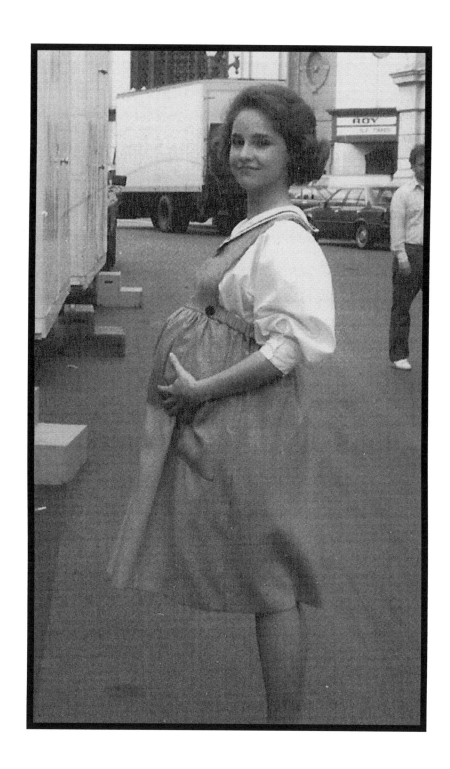

Guest Star Roles

So, it was back to L.A. for auditions. I was still not convinced that living in Los Angeles was the best move, but there was so much work there that I had to put college on hold and give it a try.

I want to make a point here that an acting career is not linear. That is to say, it's not like you get a master's degree and now you can simply get a job as an actor. It is the career of a maverick. You have to think outside the box, be flexible, and be able to ride the wave of uncertainty. This is why, even though many people wish to be actors, they may not have the personality for it.

In my case, because I started so young, I was able to save my money and live off it during my down time. If I had not done this, I would have probably gotten a job as a waitress to support my vision.

I was now over 21, I had an apartment in Venice, a car, was independent, well prepared, had great representation, but I still had to be on my toes. During this time I must have gone on five auditions a week. But unlike a lot of actors, I actually enjoyed auditioning. I didn't wait for a job to commit. I treated each audition like I already had the part, and I just became the character. It was fun.

But there were months where, no matter how hard I tried, I couldn't get work. I never stopped believing in myself, but at times it was disheartening. The acting profession demands loving the life of an actor. It is freelance. It is spontaneous and takes a lot of patience and self-motivation.

Just like in dating, I couldn't expect to attract someone if I was desperate or self-loathing. It was not the responsibility of the people who cast me to feed me. They wanted to hire someone who was autonomous, in a good head, and not needy. Not everyone can think this way. This is why not everyone is cut out to be a working actor.

Although there were many parts I wish I had gotten, I never took rejection personally. I knew that the chances to get work depended on several things. I needed to be right for the role, there were internal politics, there was chemistry between everyone that had to work, and I had to really *want* the role (it might be a great character, but not a great project). If I had ever thought of auditioning in terms of being personally rejected, I could never have handled the life of an actress.

Yet, living in Los Angeles took time to get used to. I don't think a day went by that I didn't consider moving back to New York. The only thing that kept me there was my love of acting and the belief in myself to have something worthwhile to share with audiences. I felt that if I had something I could do and something I could say better than anyone else, and if I had no fear to express it, then success would find me. I just had to be brave enough to show my individual voice and not worry what others thought. I couldn't be concerned with social norm.

My best acting comes when I am totally focused on the work. Being in the scene is more important to me than getting the job, more important than showing I can act, or being afraid. The real feeling of acting is when I don't know what I did, meaning I was just in the moment.

I started to work again in the fall of 1983. I recurred on two TV shows at the same time, both for NBC, and both as love interests.

I was a different guy's girlfriend every other week. One week, I was Tom Byrd's sweetheart, on the television series *Boone* wearing straight hair and speaking in a Southern accent, playing alongside awesome Jennifer Tilly (interestingly, Jennifer's sister Meg was the original Constanze in *Amadeus*). The next week, I was Tony Spiridakis' crush on the TV drama *Bay City Blues*, playing a back East baseball team owner's daughter, who gets involved with one of the players

While *Bay City Blues* did not last, I have fond feelings for the show. I am privileged to have worked for Steven Bochco (*Hill Street Blues, NYPD Blue*) and Jeffrey Lewis (*Hill Street Blues, Glory and Honor*). They put a lot of heart into that show. Yet, I always wondered how NBC hired me to play both roles at the same time. I guess nobody noticed.

In 1985, I appeared in *Finder of Lost Loves* as Emily Bennett, a redheaded pregnant teen. I also appeared in *The Insiders* as a young woman whose husband was in the hospital. The interesting thing about the latter role was that it was the first time I didn't play a teen. My hair was shorter after playing Monique in *Better Off Dead*, and I was being finally being considered for more character roles.

One of those roles was young Amanda Ewing in the TV movie *Dallas: The Early Years*. Without even auditioning, I was cast and flown to Dallas, Texas, to portray this young woman with a Texas accent living in an insane ward, and I had to sing "Poor Butterfly." It was a thrill to do a character as an adult woman and to be part of the *Dallas* television legacy.

Dallas: The Early Years as young Amanda Ewing

But my teen roles were not over yet.

In 1987, I played Scott Baio's Yugoslavian girlfriend, Anna Grudov, on the sit-com *Charles in Charge*. I loved the role because I got to do comedy, use another accent, work with Scott Baio (*Happy Days*) and Willie Aames (*Eight is Enough*), and I got to meet Ken Mars (*The Producers*).

Scott and Willie made every scene fun—on screen and off. They had great energy, comic timing, and wonderful physicality. But what made the episode really special for me was working with Scott Baio. I grew up watching him as Chachi on *Happy Days* so I felt like I already knew him. *Happy Days* was an institution at my home. I'd race home to see it because there was no way to record it at the time, and watch him every week. It was incredible for me to think I was now playing opposite him! It was truly a blast to work with him and seduce him in the episode!

Another thrill was playing Ken Mars' Yugoslavian daughter. I remember Ken from *The Producers,* and I thought he was an amazing actor. He loved using different dialects as I did, and he whole-heartedly committed to his characters. I really respected his talent. The episode we did together went so well that there was talk of having us back.

In the end, however, Scott Baio's character needed to date different women. Part of the show's appeal was keeping Charles in charge . . . and single.

That year, I also worked on the show *Matlock* as Nancy Lamont, an army wife, in a two-part episode called the "Court Marshal." I got to meet Andy Griffith, which was exciting because, growing up, I also watched *The Andy Griffith Show* (another family institution).

Matlock was great fun because I was being cast as a young woman, a part that somewhat carried over into my role of Jessica in "The Bride Wore Red" from the *Freddy's Nightmares* television series in 1988. Jessica was a exciting to play, but freaky to watch. Dying is one thing, but being cut in half with a chainsaw is another. Though it was not graphic, it was definitely unsettling. Fans of horror certainly enjoy it.

Around the same time, I went to Utah to work on *Encyclopedia Brown*, playing the part of a young woman in "The Case of the Ghostly Rider." I got to work with Savage Steve Holland again, who was generous enough to cast me . . . again.

I felt excited to work with Taylor Negron on *Encyclopedia*, who played the unbelievably funny, careless, and sleazy mailman in *Better Off Dead*. This was the first time we actually met since we had no scenes together in *BOD*.

I always thought Taylor was wonderfully understated. He constantly made me laugh with his line readings. My favorite sequence with him in *Encyclopedia* was the sepia flashback in the saloon, when we were all dressed in old-fashioned western garb. I was able to live out my *Little House on the Prairie* fantasy playing a schoolmarm.

In 1989, I flew to Toronto, Canada, to play a ditzy, futuristic secretary named Paulette in *Alfred Hitchcock Presents*. I wore acrylic nails, overly tight clothes, and I had really big hair. I loved playing this role because the character was so over the top and hopelessly clueless.

One of my favorite scenes in the show was when comedian/actor Rich Hall, who plays a scientist, explains to me what a book is. The scene was brilliantly simple and foreboding. And now with kindle, it seems to be coming true!

The sets were wonderfully futuristic, and the script was brilliant. I felt very fortunate to be part of the Alfred Hitchcock series.

In 1991, I played Phyllis Gant, a rich, spoiled brat in the classic television series *Murder, She Wrote*, a show that was made popular in the 80s. When the network offered me the role, I knew my career was taking another turn. I didn't even have to audition. That's because the producers weren't necessarily hiring me for my talent. They were hiring me mostly for my name. Now, that may sound like the ultimate dream, but it felt strange.

Not auditioning for the role just felt wrong. To me, the audition process is invaluable. It's the time to bring the character to life and define it for the producers. Without the audition, the *Murder, She Wrote* people would never know what I had planned for the character. So I had no idea if my take on the role of Phyllis was what they were looking for.

The audition process has other benefits as well. During the 80s, I got a part as a regular on a television show called *AfterMASH*—no audition on this one, either. I was to play the character Klinger's girlfriend. I had grown up watching *MASH* and was thrilled with the possibility of working with such talented actors. Well, when I walked on set, everyone quietly freaked out. I still remember their frozen faces and the whispering that followed.

Then, when the director and producers actually saw me next to Jamie Farr in person, they politely told me they made a mistake—I looked much too young to be play his girlfriend. Jamie was in his 40s at the time and, although he looked great, I have to say I kind of agreed that we didn't pair up well.

But television was not meant to be my claim to fame. During the 80s, my most recognizable medium was film.

80s Films

The Last American Virgin (1982)

RATED R
No one under 17 admitted
without an adult

Karen

My first film role was to play Karen in *The Last American Virgin*. It was winter of 1981. I was 18, and had just enrolled in my second semester at NYU when I got the call to meet the producers.

Initially, I turned down the audition because it directly conflicted with my chemistry midterm. Upon getting into the exam, however, I realized I had a better chance of getting a lead in a movie than passing the midterm.

A few minutes into my test, I jumped out of my seat, got on the subway, and made my way to the audition. I did not straighten my hair that day because I had "booked out" and did not intend to meet anyone. But in that one moment while taking that chemistry test, I changed my mind, and found myself reading for Cannon Films producers, Golan, and Globus an hour later.

They must have liked what they saw because they asked me to fly to California immediately to screen test for the role of Karen. It all happened very fast and, frankly, if I was a chemistry whiz, it might not have happened at all.

Within a week, I was flying to L.A. to meet the writer-director, Boaz Davidson. The producers put me up in the Holiday Inn, off Sunset in Hollywood, which to me, at the time, was the most wonderful place in the world.

Boaz was very nice and open to my suggestions. I remember thinking that I would talk to him about changing the ending of the script, which was, well . . . very sad. That's when I learned I was the actress, not the writer.

The story was a remake of a series of successful Israeli films called *Lemon Popsicle,* and it was also based on the director's life. But to me, *Virgin* had two very opposite tones in the story. I remember having mixed feelings about that. One minute it was this raucous sex comedy, and the next it was this gritty, real, heartfelt story. The tonal change was so drastic that it took me by surprise.

But there was also something about it I really liked, something that drew me to it: the reality of the story. So I just committed to doing my job as an actress, making my character as believable as possible.

When I entered the Cannon office on Hollywood Boulevard, I remember how excited everyone was to meet me. I met Boaz, his wife, Bruria (also the editor), and the producers again. But I didn't even have the role. I was going up against another actress from New York. He name was Kristian Alfonso (*Days of Our Lives*), and she was a very beautiful actress with that Brook Shields look—dark eyebrows and wavy hair.

When I walked into the casting office, I saw her headshot hanging next to mine. If I got the role, I was expected to stay and start shooting immediately. If I didn't, I was to return to New York.

Boaz asked me to read with three actors—newcomer Lawrence Monoson (*Mask*), Steve Antin (*The Goonies*), and one other actor for the part of Gary. After going back and forth, reading with each actor, Boaz finally told me I got the part. I couldn't believe it! It was the closest thing to experiencing overnight success.

Being the lead in a feature film was only a dream until now. Shortly after I got the part, I found out that Lawrence and Steve were cast as well. We were all really happy.

Here with my first feature film director, Boaz Davidson

Last American Virgin 80s fashion

Right away, I was introduced to Brian Peck (*Return of the Living Dead*) and Kimmy Robertson (*Honey, I Shrunk the Kids*), who played the best friends. They were really nice, and extremely funny.

We were sent right away to wardrobe to do a mix-and-match fashion show for Boaz so he could decide what we would all wear for the film. It was that quick.

But I had a problem. How could I rationalize my character's choices in the script? She was the total opposite of me philosophically. I would never treat a guy that callously or do what she did at the end of the film.

Then, the director showed us *Lemon Popsicle*, film that *Virgin* was based on, and I saw the actress who played the part. She was just a girl—not a mean girl, or an evil girl, but just a girl. And it occurred to me that Karen was one of those people who is extremely un-opinionated and just reacts to the moment. She has no center, no self, no identity. She gravitates to whomever is nicer to her in the moment, like a feather in the wind. I now knew how to play her.

Another aspect of the film that made me a bit nervous was the required nudity. This was my first lead role in a film, and I was thrilled. I knew I could play the part, but I was concerned about doing nudity and if it was the right choice for my career.

When an actress agrees to do nudity, it sets off a tumbling effect. I would now be offered more roles with nudity, and perhaps be branded as "the girl who takes off her clothes." I remember thinking that my choice to do a nude scene wouldn't just affect me. It would also affect those around me. I know it sound crazy, but I actually considered all this.

Prior to leaving for California, I discussed the situation with my family, who didn't have a problem with it because they had a more open European perspective about nudity. In their opinion, it was natural and beautiful. They felt as long as doing the film made me happy, it was worth it.

They also realized that this was an opportunity for me to break into the film world, and that opportunities like that don't come to everyone. I had to decide for myself what I felt comfortable doing. I felt that as long as the nudity was an integral part of the story, I would do it.

It was ironic, however, that I was hired to play a nude scene as a passive, vulnerable girl because I had to be such an independent, self-sufficient, strong female in real life to do it. Yet, my desire to become a professional actress and support myself was a priority in my life.

I met actor Joe Rubbo, who played the role of David, and his mom at the beach. We had literarally a day to site see and acclimate ourselves to L.A. I have fond memories of working with Joe, especially in the party scene. When Kimmy slapped him at the dance, it was just so funny. He took a lot of abuse, but never complained. We didn't have a lot of scenes together, but we had a lot of fun.

I also remember enjoying my rides to and from set. Although, I had just turned 19 when we actually started filming I still couldn't rent a car, and certainly didn't know L.A. at all, so the producers provided me with a driver that would take me all around the city during my visit.

And then there was the role itself. I really did enjoy playing Karen. She could just be. She didn't have to do anything to have Gary fall in love with her. She was the object of his love. Personally, I couldn't just play her as a silly little girl. At the end, I wanted to show that she grew up a little. She knew what love was, but just wasn't strong enough to stand up for it.

In that last scene of the film, I paid homage to my first love. Walking away from someone you love is one of the most painful and gripping things you can do. I was thinking of the first person I fell in love with. And the tears just fell.

I always thought that no matter what happened with *Virgin*, I at least put something authentic in it. I felt real love, and I wanted to show it.

Sex, on the other hand, is a different story. Sex was much freer in the 80s than it is now. This was before AIDS had become so well recognized, and the worst thing a girl had to worry about was getting an STD or getting pregnant.

The Last American Virgin cast

Diane Franklin, Steve Antin, Joe Rubbo, Lawrence Monoson, Kimmy Robertson and Brian Peck

Personally, I didn't have a problem with the sex in the film. I was a sensual person and felt comfortable expressing myself with my body. In my opinion, the fact that I was thought to be under age was more controversial.

In real life, I didn't have sex until I was 18. Growing up, I didn't know many girls who had. To me, the age thing was more film exaggeration than the truth. It was more exciting to write about a girl under 18 having sex than one that was over 18.

Still, young girls do feel sexy and they do go through a sexual awakening. For this reason, *The Last American Virgin* really lets girls see that even nice girls get pregnant.

The sex scene with me was hypnotic and fantasy based. It's what sex should feel like when you're falling in love—slow and gentle. Karen is falling in love for the first time with Rick.

The night we shot the scene, I was definitely hesitant. I had never shot a nude scene before and didn't know what to expect. There are so many other actresses who have a better body than I do. I was kind of surprised they gave me the part, especially since no one had ever seen or even asked to see what my body looked like nude before. For all I knew, I could get to the set, take off my shirt, and find them saying, "We're sorry, this is just not going to work out."

But that's not what happened.

The high school football field was black, except for a lit-up room at the top of the stands where camera lights blared.

Earlier that day, Steve Antin posed for pictures by the bleachers for publicity. A lot of the cast and crew were now being told to leave the area because it was going to be a "closed set."

Only a handful of people were allowed to stay for scene prep. And even then, once make-up, hair, lighting, and sound were finished, anyone who was not integral to shooting the scene was asked to stand outside the tiny announcer's box.

So there I was with the director, the cameraman, and Steve, waiting to shoot my first nude scene. With clothes on, Boaz first gave us direction on what he wanted us to do—where we move, who does what.

I was nervous, but Boaz and Steve were very reassuring and professional. Once we figured out everything in rehearsal, it was time to do the real thing. The way it was blocked, I would face away from Steve when he took off my shirt. This felt a little unnatural, but was better for camera. The room was darkly lit and very quiet, except for Boaz who was giving us directions when to move.

We started the scene kissing, and then, there I was lifting off my shirt. I have to say it was kind of anti-climactic, kind of like a guy lifting off his shirt. Nobody said "Eww" or "Wow!" It was just silent.

After Boaz called "cut," everyone started to laugh. I think they were nervous, too. They didn't know if I'd freak out or what I'd look like. Getting that first shot made everyone relax.

Then it became technical. We had to do the bit over and over again for close-ups and different angles until it was done. There was no romantic music and no cozy atmosphere. It was just Steve and I making out on a hard cold table, with a cameraman watching us, and a director calling "cut" every few minutes.

The scene only took about a half an hour to shoot, and when it was done, I felt exhilarated. I couldn't believe I did it. More than that, I felt happy that it was a professional experience. It didn't get weird.

What about the chemistry between Steve and me? On-screen it was great. Steve is very sexy and charming. I could really be free with him, improvising and getting into character. In real life, I remember so many girls having crushes on him. He's a very smart and confident guy, with a great sense of humor. We became good friends, but that's as far as it went.

The same went for Lawrence Monoson, who played Gary. I thought Lawrence was a sweetheart, but we didn't have a lot of time to socialize, except when we were on set. He was the youngest of us all and worked really hard on his role as the lead. We never knew it, but he was only 17.

The whole cast of *Virgin* bonded as good friends because it was basically our first film. We remain friends to this day.

Virgin brought up another issue that was reflective of 80s culture: abortion.

During the 1980s, although not a desired situation, abortion was a more practiced, more common, and more acceptable option for women when they got pregnant. The abortion scene in *Virgin* was probably early sex education for a lot of people on the consequences of pregnancy. The act of abortion was not as controversial as it is today.

I, personally, did not have a problem with acting out the abortion scene at the time, as I was the actress, not the writer. The biggest problem with the abortion scene to me was not the choice, but the fantasy of how easy it is for the woman to go through an abortion. Whenever I see my giggling smile after the procedure, I think how the audience might feel that abortion is a piece of cake. This is obviously not true.

The film did, however, show that a young girl could recover from abortion and move on. What is essential about the scene itself is that my character doesn't make a big deal about the *choice* of abortion, like one might do today. Karen exemplifies the 80s way of thinking for young women—independent and without guilt. I can only say that, in playing Karen, I tried to be as sincere and heartfelt as I could in her difficult situation.

On the lighter side, there was one thing I could not do (or at least admit I could not do until I made it to the set), and that was ride a bike. This was due to the deafness in my right ear affecting my balance. Many people tried to teach me the art of balancing on two wheels. I always wound up careening into a tree or I'd just hit the asphalt.

It's funny how everyone assumes you can ride a bike. When I read the script where my character rides in and out of scenes, I cringed. I decided rather than make a big deal about it, I was better off to bring this up on the set.

We were shooting the first scene the fast-food restaurant. I figured that was as good a time as ever to tell the director I couldn't do it. He was surprised. But he worked around it. For every scene I had to ride a bike or moped, Boaz had me walk it out of frame. He was really a cool director.

Memorable scenes to shoot were the party scenes. It was just great to work with the entire cast and the extras. There is something so exciting about getting a group of actors together. One minute everyone's chatting, in their own world, the next minute we hear the word "action" and everyone is unified in one action.

We shot the party scenes at a private home in L.A., which was decorated in colorful 80s decor. We shot both the early party and the end party scenes at the same time and I distinctly remember that the clothes we all wore were definitely 80s, but unique. I loved the way they took advantage of my curly locks and put tons of little bows in it. It was a creative atmosphere for everyone and Boaz was open to others ideas.

Diane Franklin, Steve Antin, Kimmy Robertson and Lawrence Monoson

There was a pretty blond girl, named Julie, who played an extra in that scene who told me how much fun she had shooting the party scenes. Years later, we met again because our daughters went to the same school and became good friends. Small world.

My favorite scene from *Virgin* was the last scene. To me, that was the most heartfelt part of the film and an unforgettable moment. Whether you hate me or love me, one never forgets that moment. It is so real and raw. The ending of the movie is an iconic example of 80s culture. It combines fantasy with gritty reality, which is what 80s culture was all about.

Although *Virgin* will always be referred to as a 80s sex comedy, I will always think of *Last American Virgin* as something so much more.

Amityville II: The Possession (1982)

RATED R
No one under 17 admitted
without an adult

Patricia Montelli

It was the fall of 1981 when I was asked to audition for the part of the daughter, Patricia Montelli, in *Amityville II: The Possession*. I was still 19.

I had returned to New York to take another semester at NYU when I got the call. I thought the chances of my getting the film were pretty slim. I was nothing like the character, and nobody knew about *The Last American Virgin* yet, so I thought, *I'll just go in and do a good read for the casting director*.

But when I got a callback, I had to take the role much more seriously. To be honest, when I got the script, I wasn't thrilled about the nudity again. It's not that it was shameful. I just didn't want to be continually cast as the girl who did nudity. I felt I had a lot more to offer.

What *did* get me to want to play the part were a few other factors. It would be the first time I got to do a horror film, which I always wanted to experience as an actress. And I liked that the film was based on a true story, which took place near where I grew up.

It also happened to be a golden opportunity to work with some very gifted actors. Burt Young (*Rocky*) and James Olson (*Commando*) had already been set to do the film. Of course, my manager advised me that the part could lead to better roles. I took that with a grain of salt, and went for the callback.

With fabulous irony, my main competition was Elizabeth Berridge, who years later won her role in *Amadeus*. We both screen-tested, and it was very close. It was the first time we went up for the same role and I was kind of surprised. We were very different in looks, voice and in energy. Only our height and hair color were similar.

Regardless, this time I was chosen for the part, and I eventually agreed to do it.

I was very excited to be in a horror film, especially this one, because I grew up near the town of Amityville. I took the next semester off from school, and went on a scary adventure instead.

We began shooting the exteriors of the film first, which was oddly not done in Long Island, but in Tom's River, New Jersey. The house looked almost identical to the original Amityville home in Long Island, and had a very eerie feel.

It was cold and bleak during the month of March 1982, and everyone on the film crew worked quickly and quietly. It was much more of an intense feeling on the set than *Virgin*, and I think the director, an Italian filmmaker named Damiano Damiani (*A Bullet for the General*), ran it that way for a reason. He was a demanding director with a vision.

My favorite shot outside in New Jersey was the body bag scene. I got to wear pale make-up, get zipped up in a body bag, and play dead. It was seriously so much fun.

Jack Magner (*Firestarter*) was very nice, but he stayed more to himself because of the intensity of his role. Rutanya Alda (*The Deer Hunter*) and I became friends because she played my mom and we had so many scenes together. In real life she was a very warm and caring person. She played the perfect "worried mother" opposite Burt Young's role as tyrannical dad.

Burt Young was an intense actor, but was also really funny. He taught me a lot about acting, and we became very close as well.

James Olson and I didn't have many scenes together, but he was very professional and sweet.

In general, everyone in the film stayed slightly in character on and off-screen—we didn't get too close while working to keep the estranged relationship dynamics going.

A few weeks later, we shot the interiors in a sound stage in Mexico City. One of the interesting things about making a horror film is that it really isn't that scary while you're working on it. So while there may be lots of screaming and special effects during production, the real frightening parts come from music and sound effects. That's when your skin crawls.

I remember watching the dailies and thinking, *How is this clock scary?* or, *What is so frightening about a close-up of the stairs?* I learned a horror film really comes to life in post-production.

Mexico City is where I did most of my crying and screaming. I cried and screamed so much so that I developed a shock of gray hair that I have to this day.

Yet, one day I ran out of tears. Director Damiano Damiani had me run around the inside of the church to get my emotions up right before we shot the confession scene. It was a really smart idea on his part because it physically shook me up and made me out of breath for the scene where I had to confess my sins to the priest.

And then came the incest scene.

The incest scene is one of the most unsettling parts of the film, not only because of Sonny's actions, but also because of my character's reaction. We understand that the devil is making him do it, but why doesn't my character scream and fight?

Once again, this was not my call. My job was to act and justify the situation. The only way I could make my character believable was to assume I was so sheltered by my family and religious upbringing that I did not have the knowledge or confidence to stop it. Therefore, I went into a sort of trance-like feeling, like, *This isn't really happening, I'm helpless, if I yelled no one would believe me anyway.*

I know the "male fantasy" aspect of the scene is that Patricia enjoyed it. There's the gritty reality of the 80s meets fantasy again. Whatever the audience wants to believe is their choice. I only know that after that scene, I am torn between protecting my brother and fearing him. Patricia Montelli personifies the ultimate victim, the kind that keeps secrets.

Incest, obviously, is a serious issue. No one should be forced to have sex under any circumstances, but playing this scene was more awkward than taboo.

Personally, I really struggled with trying to make the scene as realistic as possible. My character was written to be so naive, but it just didn't seem real to me. I had to find a way to make my lines sound as natural as possible, so I played Patricia with as much innocence as possible.

Amityville II: The Possession
Erika Katz, Ratanya Alda, Burt Young, Jack Magner, Diane Franklin and Brent Katz

Like *Virgin*, we had a closed set on *Amityville* when we were filming the nudity. Jack Magner was trying to stay in character and everything got real quiet. We did the bit where I undress in a single shot. I heard no gasps or fanfare, just silence.

Unfortunately, there were no laughs between shots either. The feeling in the room was of serious business. The crew stayed somber because they wanted to keep the mood of the scene. It wasn't bad. It just wasn't fun.

Then, after shooting the scene, I was told that the producer, Dino De Laurentiis (*La Strada*, *Serpico*, *Hannibal*), wanted to meet with me right away. He called me into the front seat of his stretched limousine parked outside the Mexican sound stage, and he asked me, very nicely, if I could go from partial nudity to total nudity for the incest shot. He said the body is a beautiful thing and that there was nothing wrong with it. He had the European sensibility I had been raised with.

Mr. De Laurentiis did what any good producer does—he tried to get the most for his film. But here I was, now 20 years old, alone in Mexico, having to discuss my naked body with one of the most renowned producers in the world. There was much more to the job of acting than just playing the role. It required knowing how to handle oneself in business situations, without freaking out.

Luckily, all my previous work experience prepared me for this uncomfortable situation. I told Mr. De Laurentiis that I didn't feel comfortable doing total nudity, and that I was sticking to what I signed in my original contract, which was partial nudity only.

And that was that. I'm sure that wasn't what Mr. De Laurentiis wanted to hear, but he accepted my refusal and was very gracious about it.

What I did like about shooting *Amityville* was working with professionals, traveling to another country, and getting to haunt as a ghost. Acting in this film was certainly an adventure.

Second Time Lucky
(1983)

RATED R
No one under 17 admitted
without an adult

Eve

One of the worldliest adventures I have ever had the pleasure of experiencing was the film *Second Time Lucky*. This movie was the story of Adam being tempted by Eve throughout time. Although playing Eve was, once again, revealing, at least this time the nudity was true to character and the rewards of playing the role were astounding.

I auditioned for *Second Time Lucky* in L.A. when I was 21. I met Oscar-nominated English director Michael Anderson (*Around the World in 80 Days*) for the first time.

Michael was a soft-spoken man who clearly loved the project. He was very interested in having me play the part of Eve. He assured me that the nudity would be done tastefully, that the cast would include some well-known English actors, including esteemed dancer Sir Robert Helpmann (*The Red Shoes*) playing the Devil, and Robert Morley (*Beat the Devil*) playing God. The movie would be shot in New Zealand.

Michael really didn't have to convince me. The role of Eve was amazing. It was actress paradise, and I said yes immediately.

A week later I flew to Auckland, New Zealand, where I was to spend a month filming.

When I got off the plane, I was greeted with a little surprise.

I was immediately detained by customs. They went through my bags and asked why I was in New Zealand, who was waiting for me, and what I did for a living. Then came the strip search.

I had absolutely no idea what was going on. No one was telling me anything, and I was alone. They wouldn't even let me contact the film company people who I was supposed to meet.

Then customs finally told me that they thought I was smuggling drugs into the country because I slept all the way on the flight without eating or drinking anything, and that I was also suspect because I was an actress from Los Angeles.

I laughed. Of all the people in the world, no one knows less about drugs than I do. I've never taken drugs, let alone smuggled them.

Of course, customs didn't find it very funny. I had to tell them why I slept during the whole flight—I knew with the time difference and arriving in the morning, I would have to sleep the entire 16-hour flight so I'd be fresh to work.

After the hour-long interrogation, they finally let me go.

When I arrived at my hotel, the production company had a big bouquet of flowers in my room to apologize for the inconvenience. It was an unusual arrival to a country, but I was still glad to be there. And the best was yet to come.

Getting a chance to work with Michael Anderson was incredible. He was a gracious and sensitive director with an amazing aesthetic eye. He had a vision, and he knew how to capture it on film. He made each era look so authentic that I really felt like I was living in a different time.

I also felt so very fortunate to work for him. He had worked with some of the greatest actresses of all time, including Sophia Loren, Elizabeth Taylor, Natalie Wood, and Olivia de Havilland. He said that, as an actress, I was absolutely in their caliber as a leading lady. He told me I really knew how to use the camera, and that I had beauty that reminded him of Elizabeth Taylor. Wow! I felt flattered that someone with his experience saw me in that kind of light.

The first scenes we shot were in the Garden of Eden, and that meant it was time to do nudity. If any scene justified baring it all, that was it.

And yet, when I was interviewed for the role, I was not asked to take my clothes off so they could see what I looked like. In fact, I have never been asked to take off my clothes for any audition, except one time when director Sergio Leone (*A Fistful of Dollars*, *The Good, The Bad, and the Ugly*) was looking for a young girl to be in a bathing scene to double as young Elizabeth McGovern in the epic film *Once Upon a Time in America*.

Usually producers just ask me if I had any scars, piercings, or tattoos. Then they hope for the best when it comes time to shoot the scene. Nudity in the business is treated in a very respectful and professional manner.

The Garden of Eden scenes may have been idyllic on screen, but they were comical in execution. It was summer in New Zealand, but the stream water was still freezing. I remember frolicking in my birthday suit with a teeth-chattering smile, as guys wearing full wet suits stood next to me to keep me from falling in. My leading man in the film, Roger Wilson (*Porkys*) was kind enough to wear as little as possible during our nature scenes, but it was far from being romantic.

Imagine two people dressed in slippers, throwing robes on and off between shots, acting with a man dressed as a snake, surrounded by bright lights, sound equipment, a film camera, and a New Zealand crew of about 50. It was not very intimate.

My favorite moment was when a group of unsuspecting tourists strolled by while we were shooting. They stood for a moment with their mouths open until production ushered them away. It was a priceless moment.

As Eve in the Garden of Eden

Yet, even with all those people around, I felt very natural to be naked in this botanical wonderland. My sense of relaxation and physical freedom not only came from being in a foreign country, in such a beautiful green setting, but also from shooting a scene with no sexual energy. Roger and I were like two kids running around naked under a sprinkler. It was just plain fun.

Working with Roger was wonderful, but initially awkward. He is extremely handsome and very sweet, but I felt our chemistry was not clicking. I'm not sure why, but we just weren't in sync off camera.

With Roger Wilson playing 1920's Detective Adam and I as Evie

That was actually a good thing, though. My rule of thumb is not to mix business with pleasure. I have never dated anyone during a shoot because off-screen romance kills on-screen chemistry. The most exciting part of attraction is watching the energy *before* something happens. I personally like to keep the heat for the film.

As Roger and I did more scenes together, the work flowed and we became good friends. We also became Caesar and Cleopatra, a French nurse and an English soldier in WWI, a gangster girlfriend and a detective from the 1930s, and futuristic punk rock singers—the all-in-one movie!

Every time period was an incredible experience, but the scenes we did at the speakeasy were my favorite. Something about being a platinum blond with blond-dyed eyebrows was an eye-opening experience. Not only was the chemistry on between Roger and me in the scene, but my new look affected the crew's reaction as well.

I remember a couple of guys treating me as if I was helpless and as if I didn't have a brain in my head. It was so surprising how something as simple as hair color could affect how others treated me.

After we completed *Second Time Lucky*, I flew back to Los Angeles, only to find I had another amazing adventure waiting for me.

I had to fly to Melbourne, Australia, to do the looping (voice-over) for the film. I was stunned I got to travel again. And this time Down Under!

After the voice session, I visited Sydney, and stayed with the make-up artist from the film. I saw the play *I.Q.* at the Sydney Opera House and tried vegemite, which I have to admit . . is not my favorite food.

Second Time Lucky was the first film I received top billing. And while the enticement of nudity was a big selling point, it didn't stop me from showing off what I could do as an actress.

Essentially, *Second Time Lucky* was the golden opportunity for me to explore comedy and character. It gave me the chance to stretch my acting ability, and be creative. It also instilled in me a sense of confidence portraying a French woman, which turned out to be just what I needed to play a French-exchange student in an upcoming comedy.

Better Off Dead (1985)

RATED PG
Parental Guidance Suggested Some
material may not be suited for
children

Monique Junet

The funniest film I have ever had the privilege of working on was *Better Off Dead*! Hands down, Savage Steve Holland is the most wonderful and inspired comedic filmmaker of the 80s. His film, *BOD* was just genius. It had a groundbreaking script, a true visionary at the helm, a beautiful filming location, and true chemistry between the cast and crew.

Savage called me in to read for the part of Beth after seeing me in *The Last American* Virgin, but I had my eye on the character Monique. I had just done a French accent in *Second Time Lucky*, and I was absolutely confident about playing the French exchange student.

I adored the script, and I was thrilled to be up for a part where I didn't have to bare all. My first thought after reading the script was, *WOW!! Finally a movie I would want to see! It's sweet, it's funny, and it's like nothing I've ever seen.*

I knew I could make Monique realistic, as well as endearing, and I hoped Savage could see this in me as well. I met him and producer Michael Jaffe in a small office in L.A. when they asked me to read for the part of Beth. I did my best with the lines, but I really had my heart set on Monique.

There is something magical that happens when an actor connects to a character. There is no trying, no tension or neediness in the room. Suddenly, the actor disappears, and only the character is in the room. I got a chance to read lines for Monique. Afterward, I continued my conversation with Savage and Michael with a French accent—as Monique. They started to laugh and relax. They could see I owned the character.

Savage then directed me to try for a French accent with a lisp to make the character more adorable. It didn't work, but he was able to see how well we worked together.

I felt good when we all shook hands at the end of the audition, and I said *au revoir* to Savage and Michael on my way out. I went home hoping it would work out.

The next day, I got the call. I got the part as Monique Junet.

Oh mon dieu!

With comic genius filmmaker, Savage Steve Holland

In the mid-80s, I finally got to play a character that was a positive female role model—Monique was a strong, opinionated girl with a firm grip, who could inspire John Cusack's character to be brave enough to ski the K12. I knew this was going to be a great adventure.

Playing the French exchange student Monique Junet was a dream. How often did a teen girl, in the 80s, play a smart and funny love interest? A character as quirky as Monique would normally be seen as the sidekick, not the leading lady.

Additionally, Monique's fashion style was masculine, yet I was still feminine. This harkens back to Diane Keaton's look from *Annie Hall*—oversized coat, men's hat, and layering with vests. In the 80s, Monique could play this with confidence, not neurosis.

Attractiveness took the form of a cute Groucho Marx, and sexiness took the form of spirit. Monique was a true progressive role model for the 80s girl, and I was lucky that Savage considered me for the role.

Working with the cast of the film was amazing. Every actor Savage hired was a consummate professional. They each had the confidence to take their role one step further than the script. That's because Savage really made the cast feel comfortable, and he encouraged them to do a little improvising. Vincent Schiavelli was masterful at this. His performance made a typical classroom scene priceless. Coincidently, I had met Vincent before, on the Prague set of *Amadeus*. I knew we were meant to work together!

Savage is always open to funny ideas, which is what makes him an inspired writer/director. He does not come from his ego. He comes from his heart. We all stuck to the script, but added little things along the way. I added some French cursing and dialogue to the ball-throwing scene because Monique would get mad in her native language. I also suggested to be blindfolded when Lane leads me into the burger restaurant, and Savage let me add it.

The blindfold made for a more amusing entrance, as well as a magical moment between Lane and Monique when he lifted it off to reveal his lovely TV dinners. This was Lane's wooing scene.

With the very wonderful and talented John Cusack

I love the scene because it is the one moment in the film where they are alone and Lane gets to reveal his love for Monique. Even though we were in a fast food restaurant and there were cold TV dinners and his saxophone playing was too loud, it was the most romantic moment in the film. Lane (and John Cusack) won my heart.

The scene was sincere and heartfelt, and that's because of John. John is a deep guy and the audience can feel it. His rendition of Lane was understated, funny, and endearing. I feel very fortunate to this day that I got a chance to work with him. John is a real sweetheart.

Another great moment I love in the film is when John and I meet in front of the high school for the first time at night. Although I had to knock John over a few times, looking into Lane's eyes was a magic moment. We had a connection there that I am happy is on film.

Then, Dan Schneider (*Head of the Class*, creator of *iCarly, Drake and Josh*), who played Ricky, runs up in all his brilliance chasing a balloon, and he reminds us once again this is a comedy. Ricky stands up to Lane and we see a brief glimpse into Ricky's authority, when his mom's not around (not even Ricky was intimidated by Lane).

The party scene was also really cool. I encouraged Dan to pick me up and throw me around the dance floor like a rag doll. He did it with ease and then busted out in his own improvised dance. Dan was fun, easy to work with, and adorable. I think we made a great comedic couple.

But the funniest scene to shoot was Christmas on the couch with Ricky and his mom. First of all I love Dan and Laura. They are wonderful actors and people. Then, I almost cried with laughter when Mrs. Smith, Laura Waterbury, (*One Crazy Summer, Honey, I Shrunk the Kids*) said *Christmas* to me and squeezed my cheeks. She's hysterical! Finally, Ricky gives me the photo of himself. Danny's subtle smile, the dancing clown doll, and the wacky photo were just cripplingly funny. It was great to be tortured by both of them!

I also adored Laura when she brought us all to tears of laughter with her loud grating nasal voice, encouraging the budding romance between Ricky and Monique with the "language of love." This was a golden moment in cinema, and I knew it. The lines were already funny, but Laura's performance knocked it out of the ballpark.

Savage did some extra takes of the scene just because we all wanted to see Laura do her dialogue again.

With brilliant actor Curtis Armstrong and anonymous hand

It was also very difficult not to laugh during the lunch scene between Danny and Curtis Armstrong (*Revenge of the Nerds*). With Dan's shy face offering me a bite of cupcake, and Curtis' innocent look in giving me the opportunity to snort some Jell-O, I really had to restrain myself from breaking out of character. No two takes were exactly alike.

Savage would just let the camera roll until someone eventually lost it—crew included. Curtis is the consummate professional, a gifted improviser, and just a lovable guy. He trusts himself, and he's not afraid to bring his own ideas to a scene.

David Ogden Stiers (*Oh, God!*, *M*A*S*H* the TV series) was very talented and fun to work with as well. In the movie, when he's grilling me at the table about how I must know some English, I actually felt like I should say something. He is a wonderful actor. (A side note: Years later, David worked on a *Mary Poppins* DVD special feature called *The Cat That Looked at the King*, which featured my 7-year-old daughter, Olivia, playing a young Jane Banks. He didn't realize we were related. Serendipity!)

It was also great to work with Kim Darby again. Yes, earlier in our relationship I drugged her, seduced her husband, and kidnapped her kids (*Summer Girl*), but now it was time to let bygones be bygones, and do some comedy. Kim was great! She is extremely smart, funny, a good sport and really sweet. During the dinner scene, we all had to control our laughter when she offered us French fries, French bread, and *Peru* (Perrier water). Her voice as the mom still makes me laugh today.

Off screen, we were all friends. We stayed at the Snowbird Resort in Utah to do the skiing shots. Aaron Dozier—the supposed ski bum—would sit with us in the lodge telling hysterical stories. He was not at all the bad guy; he was actually more of a crowd-pleaser—very social and very friendly.

With the adorable and talented Amanda Wyss at Snowbird

Amanda Wyss (*A Nightmare On Elm Street, Fast Times at Ridgemont High*) who played the character of Beth is not only beautiful and talented, but also a dear friend of mine. We met during the shoot, and remained buddies thereafter.

I remember our scene at night after the dance when Mandy walked by John and I, giving us the evil eye, it couldn't be more the opposite of her sweet personality. Amanda is simply adorable in person. I only wish we had more scenes together.

From the teacher to the mailman to the newspaper boy, Savage created such memorable characters in a world we wanted to be a part of. Savage trusted his own gut and his hired actors. He even let the director of photography, Isidore Mankofsky (*Somewhere in Time, The Muppet Movie*), who had a distinctive look, play the hedge-cutting neighbor. Savage was just like that. If he thought it was funny, he used it.

Another incredible addition to the cast of *Dead* was E.G. Daily (*Pee-wee's Big Adventure, Happy Feet*), who, in real life, is a gifted singer, actress, and voice artist. Savage hired her because he knew she was amazingly talented and, yes, hot. She was the knockout singer at the high school dance. She recorded songs for the LP and effortlessly hit the high C in the *Better Off Dead* theme song! I remember how great her voice sounded in playback during the gymnasium dance scene. Her voice made those scenes feel magical.

I am so grateful I got a chance to be in a film with E.G. because now we see each other at different *Better Off Dead* events. She's not only incredibly versatile, but also really cool as well.

The final scene I shot of the film was at Dodger Stadium. It was a beautiful day and very exciting to be out on the field. Since most of the shot was action (no dialogue), John, Savage, and I just hung out and talked while the crew set up lights and camera.

The crew was also so incredible. Everyone was really happy to work with Savage because he treated everyone with equal respect and care. Out of all the films I ever did, *Better Off Dead* had the best cast and crew chemistry by far. I think that's part of what made the movie so much fun to watch. Everybody liked working together.

Savage Steve Holland is an amazing director and writer, not just because this was his first film right out of film school, but also because he is such a funny, smart, and considerate director. Every single person on the shoot, including John Cusack, loved Savage. Yes, even John enjoyed *doing* the film.

Savage was not only constantly striving to make the scenes as funny as possible, but he was naturally funny, professional, and, what I think is more rare, completely self-effacing and endearing as a director.

Oddly, *Better off Dead*, did not do that well in theaters. Critics judged it harshly, bigger movies took the spotlight, and, thus, *Dead* never became the box office hit we all hoped it would be.

It wasn't until *Dead* hit home video and the college circuit that I heard students coming out with their love for it. From there its popularity grew. It then became a cult classic. You were "in the know" if you liked this movie.

I can only say we are all very lucky that Savage decided to be a writer/director, and say, not an accountant or dentist!. His visionary genius has affected comedy to this day in films, television series, and animation, and I am eternally grateful to be a part of his film legacy, and proud to be his friend!

Better Off Dead is an iconic 80s film that will be passed on from generation to generation because it spreads optimism and makes the world a better place to be!

Hilarious Laura Waterbury and I at Snowbird mountain before the ski pole fight scene

Terror Vision (1986)

RATED R
No one under 17 admitted
without an adult

Suzy Putterman

After *Better Off Dead*, I wanted to do more comedic roles, but such roles do not often come to ingénues.

It was difficult to find material that fit. Casting agents did not see me as a character actress, but I needed to show them I could be a character actress. That's what drew me to *TerrorVision*.

It wasn't the most sophisticated script in the world, but the role of Suzy Putterman was a chance for me to show that I could create funny characters. This, perhaps, was not the best direction for my career in terms of material, but I loved stretching myself as an actress.

I was also transitioning from playing passive female roles to playing more assertive ones. I remember once I was offered the chance to do a film that I shied away from because the character was a vulnerable, passive ingénue being stalked by a man. This film turned out to be *Smooth Talk*, which, of course, became highly acclaimed and catapulted talented Laura Dern's career. But, who's to say the movie would have been as successful if I had done the role? I think what made that film so outstanding was Laura's performance. I would not have had the same effect on the material.

I was character-driven in my career, not story-driven. Strangely, the character roles I liked emerged more in comedies rather than in drama. In *TerrorVision,* I got play a pushy, confident, outspoken caricature of a teenager. I combined a valley girl voice with a punk rock look—three wigs, tons of make-up, and lots of jewelry.

I had never played such an animated character before. Suzy Putterman was like a Japanese Anime come to life. In addition, I got to shoot a submachine gun into the water. This is not something I would normally do or recommend, but it was an adventure. So, at 24 years old, I was given another chance for creative freedom.

The biggest thrill for me was working with the cast. Mary Woronov (*Eating Raoul*), who played my mother, was a cult legend. I was also excited to work with Gerrit Graham (*Used Cars*, *Child's Play 2*), Jonathan Gries (*Napoleon Dynamite*), Bert Remsen (*Nashville*), Chad Allen (*Our House, St. Elsewhere*), Jennifer Richards (*The Tower*), and Alejandro Rey (*Moscow on the Hudson*), who I had watched growing up on the 60s TV program *The Flying Nun*. Now, that was trippy!

Jon Gries, who played my boyfriend, is talented and adorable. I loved the way he throws himself into his characters. To play O.D., he used a stoner dude voice, wore heavy metal, and played his character like Eddie Haskell meets Beavis and Butthead. O.D was funny, unique, and certainly memorable. Personally, I think Jon and I made an endearing punk couple.

The producer of the film, Charles Band (*Puppetmaster*), was awesome. No problems here. And director Ted Nicolaou (*Vampire Journals*), was a fun, easy-going and really got the genre of the movie. He made us all feel comfortable, and encouraged the cartoonish over-the-top acting style for the movie.

Now for the adventure part—we got to shoot the whole film in Rome, Italy!

I lived in a small hotel right across the street from the Trevi Fountain (made famous in Fellini's *La Dolce Vita*) for over a month. In addition, I got to bring along my boyfriend (now husband) for this adventure. He was a screenwriter at the time and could bring his work with him. It was an incredibly lucky experience for both of us.

I worked on the sound stage during the day, and walked around the streets of Rome at night. The only thing I had to pace myself with was the coffee. I love Italian coffee, but it's really strong.

So the first day of shooting I had a cup, and my hands would not stop shaking. This was a problem, considering I was in the first scene. I really had to concentrate to keep my hands still until the caffeine wore off. After that, I waited until the weekends to enjoy my cappuccino.

Working with the monster was fantastic. It was huge, and actually cute in a disgusting sort of way. The special effects guys were amazing with their puppetry, effects, and tons of slime used to create the awesome alien.

Today, a lot of monsters are added in post-production on a green screen. I thought it was so much fun to have a real monster on set to react to. The only thing I felt bad about was when the air-conditioning died in the middle of July and the goo kept melting off the monster.

I think my favorite scene in *Terrorvision* was feeding the monster junk food and it hates the food and chucks it back at us. We got covered with trash. It was so funny.

I also liked when O.D. tries to communicate with the monster. I couldn't stop laughing while we were shooting that.

Running from room to room with Sherman carrying a machine gun while trying to capture the monster was a pretty cool life experience. You just don't get to do that every day! It was all just great.

I don't know if people will be watching *Terrorvision* 50 years from now, but if they do, it will be for it's campy style, its 80s look, and the old school hand-crafted alien creature.

Bill & Ted's Excellent Adventure (1989)

RATED PG
Parental Guidance Suggested Some
material may not be suited for
children

Princess Joanna

Finally, at 25, I auditioned for what became the most commercially successful film of my career—*Bill and Ted's Excellent Adventure*.

Adventure was . . . well, an adventure from beginning to end. Originally, Dino De Laurentiis was more involved with the film, but ultimately he pulled out because he didn't understand the humor. This turned out to be a good thing, because it allowed the film to keep its offbeat sense of humor.

Alex Winter (*The Lost Boys, Freaked*) and Keanu Reeves (*The Matrix, Speed*) were set to play Bill and Ted. This was early in Keanu's career, but there was already buzz going around about his imminent success.

I was called in to audition for the part of Joan of Arc after one of the writers, Ed Solomon (*Men in Black*), recommended me for the role. Ed was a good friend of mine, so I was very grateful he suggested me, and more excited to be part of a project he was working on. I loved the Joan of Arc role, I loved the script, and I was excited to do another French accent. But the director and the producer had a different idea.

During the audition, they asked me if I could do an English accent, which I improvised immediately. It made them laugh, and so they asked me if I would be interested in playing one of the princesses. I have to admit, I was initially disappointed. Joan of Arc was a juicier role, and I thought the princess part would just go unnoticed.

But it's funny—my role as Princess Joanna (I was originally cast as Princess Elizabeth) has given me the most widespread international recognition of all my films because of its huge popularity in the 80s.

The *original* babes (Diane Franklin & Kim LaBelle), Alex Winter and the royal ugly dudes!

I did like the idea of playing a medieval princess, and using an English accent. I also looked forward to working with Keanu, Alex, and the director, Stephen Herek (*Mr. Holland's Opus*). So I agreed to do the film.

The next thing I knew, we were on our way to Rome. The castle shots were done in Bracciano, Italy, at Orsini Odescalchi Castle, and we worked there for about a week. What made it magical was the world that the production crew created. Between the castle, the costumes, medieval guillotine and all the Italian extras, it really was like stepping back in time. Bill and Ted did not fit in here. They definitely time-traveled.

Personally, the dresses were exquisite to wear, and the waist-length hair extensions were heavy, but it created the perfect medieval princess babe look. I have to say the clothes and hair reminded me of my auditions for *Amadeus*. I got to do a period piece after all. It was meant to be.

On top of all that, I got to work, playing Keanu's girlfriend. In real life Keanu was actually kind of shy with me. He shook my hand, and after that we barely spoke off screen. I don't know whether it was his busy film schedule or what, but he was more reclusive. Yet, when he was in character he was so relaxed and open as Ted. He just got into that mindset and became a dude. It was amazing to watch him. I think Bill is the most adorable character he has ever played, and personally, it is so much fun being wooed by a dude!

With the most *Excellent* Alex Winter

Alex on the other hand was very outgoing and open. He was also very creative and smart.

When we were shooting the scenes in the castle, the guys were always messing around, trying to think of funny things to add to the scene. I can see why Alex wound up becoming a director. During the shoot he seemed interested in all aspects of the film making process.

After England, the crew decided to shoot the final scene in Arizona. This was a prom scene that did not make it into the movie. The scene showed Bill and Ted in tuxedos, escorting Kim LaBelle (now Kimberley Kates) and me to the San Dimas prom. The set was complete with streamers, dance floor lighting, and tons of extras. But after seeing the dailies, the director decided the guys should remain single and focused on their music.

We re-shot the final scene in the garage of a Pacific Palisades home. This time, the very wonderful and talented comedian George Carlin escorted the princesses. George was gracious, humble, down to earth, nice, and, shall I say, clean spoken.

There is a part of George that may come out in his stand-up comedy, but around us all, he was a complete gentleman. He also plays a mean air guitar. I felt very fortunate to be able to work with him, especially since I grew up watching his stand-up routines on television as a kid. My experience with George was truly excellent!

There was talk that there may be a sequel and perhaps the babes would join the band in the next movie, but alas, *the babes* got replaced in the *Bogus Journey*. All I can guess is that the Wyld Stallyons needed to ride free! Such is the life of a babe! The funny thing about *Adventure* was that, out of all the work I have done, I get the widest recognition for my role as the princess. The film showed me that, no matter how small a role may be, if a film becomes a hit, you become a star.

How I Got Into College (1989)

RATED PG-13
Parents Strongly Cautioned Some
material may be inappropriate for
children under 13

Although *How I Got Into College* was not the final film of my career, it was the last film I did in the 80s. Savage Steve Holland was so kind to cast me again, after I wound up on the cutting room floor of *One Crazy Summer*. I walked by John Cusack at the end of the film as a wink to all the BOD fans, but Savage had to cut for time. C'est la vie! But he hired me again, this time in the role of Sharon Brown, the step-mom of the lead boy character who goes off to college in the film.

I play this way-too-young step-mom married to the father of this college-bound boy, played by Corey Parker (*Biloxi Blues*), who is eager to get him out of the house so she can take over the family. It was the hysterical idea of Savage to cast me in the role of the young mom. I look really sweet and young, but am unbelievably blunt! To this day, this role still makes me laugh, and was a fun role for me to end my decade of performing 80s entertainment!

Most Excellent Babe of the 8os?

There were many beautiful and talented teen actresses that gave memorable performances during the 80s, including Jennifer Jason Leigh (*Fast Times at Ridgemont High*), Phoebe Cates (*Gremlins*), Deborah Foreman (*Valley Girl*), Elisabeth Shue (*Adventures in Babysitting*), Molly Ringwald (*Sixteen Candles*), Ally Sheedy (*The Breakfast Club*), Laura Leigh Hughes (*Some Kind of Wonderful*), and Demi Moore (*St. Elmo's Fire*). But if you are looking for the most *excellent* babe of the 80s, you're talking about an actress who defines a look, one who has a certain energy, and a uniqueness of this much-loved era.

That's where I come in. With my dark curly hair, thick eyebrows, and Monroesque beauty mark, I had a look that was easily identifiable—a new 80s style. Even before the movie *Flashdance*, my mane hit the screen with *The Last American Virgin*, defining big curly hair as the 80s look!

The characters I played taught audiences lessons about life, whether it was learning about sex, the "language of love," or the trials and tribulations of being a teen. One of the most important things my characters did was remind people of their innocence.

Losing innocence is one of the most traumatic experiences in life. And that is why these 80s teen movies can affect us so deeply. It might be painful to lose your innocence in real life, but in film we can reflect and see an element of sweetness that I believe 80s teen films captured.

The characters I portrayed bring audiences back to a time when they can rediscover their adolescence, and remember a time of innocence. Perhaps that is why those who have seen my work are so happy to meet me. It is like they are traveling back in time and being reminded of their own naivety, vulnerability, and youth.

But the last and most important reason why I think I should be the most *excellent* babe of the 80s is that I represented a very important 80s message: Dare to be *different*! Being different was *in* during the 80s. With such entertainers as Madonna, Prince, and Cyndi Lauper, there was a newfound freedom to being unconventional.

I *am* the most *excellent* babe of the 80s because I contributed to 80s pop-culture as an actress that made *different* attractive. My presence in 80s cinema allowed the perception of the *different* teen girl to be perceived as extraordinary.

But the reason I stood out in the 80s is the same reason my career came to an end in the 90s. What makes a person popular at one time makes them unpopular at another time.

In the 90s, American girl teens became more outspoken and strong. It was no longer believable to be so helpless or gullible as a girl. This actually is a good thing. Film roles now showed girls being alert and capable, and this was empowering. The American ingénue in film changed from being passive to *prepared*. It was time to move on.

A Babe's Life in the 21st Century

Photo by Greg Crowder

So what happened to the most excellent babe of the 80s?

Well, first of all, the babe got married, which may not matter to most actresses, but for me it meant I really didn't want to make out on screen anymore. This, of course, was acting suicide.

For the previous decade, I was cast primarily as the love interest. So instead of swimming upstream trying to get character roles, I shifted my focus to having a family.

It actually worked out in an amazing way because my husband and I share the same devotion to each other as we do to our children. Together we pass on optimism and passion to our kids. We have a very creative atmosphere at home.

I am also grateful to say that I never regretted my decision to stop acting when I did, and I have been very happily married to my incredible husband, Ray, whom I love with all my heart and is *really* funny, visionary and has the biggest heart! Because of that we've been married for over 20 years.

Over the last 15 years, my main role has been MOM. Yet, unlike most parents who are actors, who typically don't want to even expose their kids to the entertainment business, I had both my kids start acting professionally when they were young. I did this for several reasons: 1) They are both actors by nature. 2) They are talented, smart, and creative. 3) They both wanted to do it!

I did not get my kids into acting because I wanted them to follow in my footsteps. I took them so they would see what the acting world was really about. So they wouldn't spend their life wondering. I can't tell you how many acting students have told me that their parents didn't want them to act, and then told me, whether their parents wanted it or not, they were going to pursue acting when they grew up no matter what! Going after your dream shouldn't be a power struggle.

But because I was a successful actress, I did not want my kids putting acting on a pedestal either. Acting was *my* dream, not theirs. I wanted them to experience the life of a performer and know what it was all about, and then make their own decisions based on the reality.

As a result, both of my kids have connected to their own aspirations, and they now pursue their own interests. My son loves music and is a gifted musician and my daughter is a filmmaker. I am beyond proud of both of them and I would personally like to go on and on about them . . . But that's another book!

I bring up my kids' aspirations because when people ask me if I am still acting, the answer is yes. I have been acting in my daughter's films!

Lass premiere with my incredible family

Dad (2012), an award-winning parody written, directed and acted by Olivia DeLaurentis & Sarah Crosthwaite. In photo: Olivia, myself and Future, the llama.

My daughter, Olivia, is a filmmaker who writes, directs, acts, and edits comedic short films. And my son, Nick, has written music, plays guitar, and he also acts in Olivia's films as well.

The Adventures of Lass, which spawned two sequels, won an award at the International Student Film Festival of Hollywood when Olivia was 12. So keep an eye out for her! In all three *Lass* films, I play two characters. I play a hard-working, always pregnant immigrant mother named MUM, and I play OLD LASS, a bi-polar, absent-minded granny. These parts are a little different than the *babe* role fans are used to.

Another role I have taken on is that of an assistant for other films my daughter has created. Her most recent comedy, which she wrote, directed and starred in (at age 15!), is called *Humanized*, which also stars Drew Cullinan, Steven Houska, and Christina Faulkner. The film not only won an award in 2011 for best romantic comedy, but has been invited to screen at the 2012 Los Angeles Film Festival!. Wish her luck!

All I can say is that I am the least talented person in the family. I feel privileged to be in my daughter's films, and lucky to have a son who plays such beautiful guitar. I am fortunate to share in their creative experiences, and grateful be part of such a loving family.

Professionally, over the years, I was able to occasionally find small roles that were more character-based. I worked on *The Big Easy, Alfred Hitchcock Presents, Family Law, Providence* as Diane Cavalero, *Hansel Meith: Vagabond Photographer* (Independent Lens), *Temptation* (onstage at the Mark Taper Forum), and *Punchcard Player*.

I've done interviews for VH1, Bravo, and ESPN Radio, and I have been included in Donruss Celebrity Trading Cards, which was such a compliment. I had no idea what picture they would choose to represent my career, and when I saw it was from *Better Off Dead,* I couldn't have been happier. That picture is totally me!

Then, in 2004, I was given the most special honor—to sing the National Anthem at Dodger Stadium. This was amazing because I not only got a chance to sing in one of the most renowned stadiums in the country, but also it brought back memories of the final location shot of *Better Off Dead*. All those years of singing lessons as a teen really paid off.

Today, I coach young professional actors, work as a drama specialist at a public school, help my daughter make her films, drive my son to basketball, tennis or music practice, attend celebrity autograph shows, care for all our animals, and spend time with my awesome family!

Of late, I haven't had much time to pursue acting professionally, but that will change. I still love to act, and am open to new experiences. So we will see what the future brings. But no matter what roles I play in the future, I know none will compare with my image in the 80s.

As an actress, I can choose my projects, but I can't choose how or if people will remember me. I'm grateful to say that I must have made a strong impression. I still get recognized to this day!

So why did I decide to write this book?

I wanted to tell my kids about my life before I was "mom," and tell my story before I forgot everything.

I wanted to say what it was really like to be an actress of the 80s, and share the knowledge of my experiences with 80s fans.

I wanted to remind people that what can seem like a burden, can be a gift and to embrace what makes you *different*!

Oh, one more thing - if I had to describe myself in one word it would be *creative*. All across the board, I love to create.

I create not for rewards, but for the sheer joy of the creative experience. Writing this book has been an example of this. It has allowed me to reflect on my wonderful career and *say* something about my life as an actress.

What I have to say is this - an acting career can be an excellent adventure after all! I say to you – be brave and have an *excellent adventure* of your own*!*

My Better Half starring Drew Cullinan (not shown),
Olivia DeLaurentis, Diane Franklin and Steven Houska (2012)

Photo by Barry King

FAN FARE

Q. *Which film or T.V. character was the most rewarding or challenging for you as an actress to play? If you were to choose another profession that was just as rewarding as acting to you, what would it be and why? - MATT COLEMAN*

A. The most rewarding character I ever played was surely Monique Junet from *Better Off Dead* because I finally got to play a character who was positive and funny. "You can do it!" should be my middle name. The most challenging character I ever played was Patricia Montelli from *Amityville II*, mostly because I was playing sort of a tomboy. I was much more comfortable playing feminine roles. As far as a different career goes, I would have chosen a vocation that involved creativity and big thinking, like a scientist, writer, inventor, artist or songwriter. I also love teaching. Working with kids has the most impact on our future, and a great teacher has a huge influence on a child's life. One occupation I would never choose is to be a chef. I like eating, but I don't like cooking!

Q. *What are you doing these days and will you make a comeback in the movie business?* – *STEPHAN HELIE*

A. Well, I've already made a comeback, but not in a traditional way. My work has been in my daughter's films. Her films are comedies, and they are truly hysterical. She has entered them in several film festivals and they have won awards. She will distribute them when the time is right. You will definitely see me work again!

Q. *Have you had any experiences in your adult life that mirrored and/or reminded you of any scene in* Better Off Dead? – *GREG ALTOBELLA*

A. Singing at Dodger Stadium definitely brought back memories of John and I sitting on the Camaro. Pretty trippy. But my favorite flashback has to be when I went skiing with my husband and kids, and I asked them what direction they were taking and my son said, "Go that way really fast. If something gets in your way, turn!" That was perfect.

Q. *When you were a teen actress, was it difficult to make and maintain friendships with schoolmates?* – *JAMES MYERS*

A. No. I was pretty friendly and made great friends who, to this day, still keep in touch. I think this is because I didn't talk about my career in school too much. I kept my school and acting separate. I loved being able to go back and forth, from a professional life to a kid life.

Q. *What was it like playing Patricia Montelli in* Amityville II: The Possession? *What was the atmosphere like in the house? How was it working with Burt Young?* – *KAMYAR PALIZI*

A. Playing Patricia was perhaps the most foreign of all the roles I've ever played because I didn't grow up with siblings, let alone have a brother. Therefore, my relationship with my brother in the film was more contrived. Because the house we shot in was not the actual Amityville house, the creepiness came from the set and situation, not the spirits. Burt Young is truly a gifted actor. He uses all his senses when he acts, is very relaxed, and knows how to get connected to his emotion. What impressed me most about him was his ability to play such intense scenes, but then in real life be so sweet, honest and funny. I loved working with him.

Q. *In the last shot of* Better Off Dead, *is that actually you and John Cusack sitting on the car at Dodger Stadium, or were doubles used? John Cusack openly shunned* Better Off Dead *immediately upon its completion and seems to consider it his least favorite film, which just seems absurd, as he is brilliant in it, and the film is truly one of the great films of the decade. Did he seem to have this opinion during the shoot, or did it manifest itself only after he saw the final edit?* – *TIM TAYLOR*

A. Yes, it was us kissing on the Camaro. As far as John shunning the film, I didn't know about it until after the cast and crew screening. I was actually really surprised. He never said a word while we were shooting.

Q. *Who would you like to work with today?* – *HEATHER WIGGINS*

A. There are so many talented people I would love to work with that it's hard to narrow down. I'd have to say I greatly admire Jemaine Clement, Bret McKenzie, Albert Brooks, Savage Steve Holland, Taika Waititi, Ben Stiller, Robert Downey Jr., Tina Fey, Jayme Lynn Evans, Will Ferrell, Jerry Trainor, Zach Mills, Woody Allen, Tom Hanks, Mitchell Hurwitz, Christopher Guest and Olivia DeLaurentis!

Q. *What other projects did you audition for?* – *JULIE HEENEY*

A. *Freaky Friday, The Exorcist, The Big Chill, The Karate Kid, Once Upon a Time in America, The Terminator, Racing with the Moon, Bachelor Party, Young Sherlock Holmes* and *Sixteen Candles* to name a few.

DIANE FRANKLIN FILMOGRAPHY

1989   *Bill & Ted's Excellent Adventure* – Princess Joanna (DEG/Orion)
        Encyclopedia Brown – "The Case of the Ghostly Rider" (HBO)
        How I Got Into College – Sharon Browne (20th Century Fox)
        Alfred Hitchcock Presents – Paulette, "Romance Machine"
        (USA Network)

1990s

1990   *Murder, She Wrote* – Phyllis Gant, "Family Doctor"
        (CBS series)
        Temptation - Lover (Mark Taper Forum. Los Angeles)

1991   *The Big Easy* (Showtime)
        Independent Lens: "Hansel Meith; Vagabond Photographer" (PBS)
        Providence –Diane Cavalero, "Blind Faith" (NBC)
        Family Law – TV Announcer, "Media Relations" (CBS)

21st Century

2000   *VH1* – 100 Funniest Movies
        Bravo
        ESPN Radio

2002   *Punchcard Player* – Sweetheart

2004   Dodger Stadium – Singing National Anthem Solo

2008   *The Adventures of Lass (Winner ISFFH Film Award)* –
        Mum/ Old Lass

2009   *The Adventures of Lass II: The Sweet Potato Rush* –
        Mum/ Old Lass
        Sketchfest, Castro Theater

2010   *The Adventures of Lass III: Going to A-Mary-Ca* – Mum/Old Lass
        That Time of the Month – Mrs. Wilson
        Toon Woof – Network President

2011   *HUMANIZED* – Computer Voice

2012   *My Better Half* – Ms. Viola Young
        TBD!

ACKNOWLEDGEMENTS

Thank you to all the studios, producers, directors, casting directors and executives who gave me the opportunity to be part of their creative vision. Thank you to all the actors/actresses I worked with, and those actresses I competed with, who helped me strive harder to become a better actress. Thank you to all the teachers and coaches who taught me skills and encouraged me. Thank you to all my agents and managers throughout the years, without whom I would not have worked at all. Thank you to all critics who reviewed my work, whether good or bad, and gave me notoriety. Thank you to all my friends and family who supported me throughout my career. And finally, thank you, fans for remembering me, even after all these years, and showing me that my performances in the 80s still withstand the test of time. THANK YOU!! I am truly grateful!

PHOTOGRAPHY CREDITS

Joseph D'Allessio
Greg Crowder
Doyle Gray
Barry King
Thomas Kriegsmann
Dan Nelken
Manny Rodriguez

Deadly Lessons, Leonard Goldberg Productions © 1983
Summer Girl, Bruce Lansbury Production / Roberta Haynes Production/Finnegan Associates/
The Summer Girl Company © 1983
Last American Virgin, Golan – Globus Productions © 1982
Amityville II: The Possession, Dino De Laurentiis Company/Media Transactions © 1982

and special thank you to Jason Simos

Printed in Great Britain
by Amazon

87701125R00077